# THE TRUTH ABOUT YOU

# THE
# Truth ABOUT
# You

*Arthur F. Miller and Ralph T. Mattson*

## TEN SPEED PRESS
*Berkeley, California*

1⊖
TEN SPEED PRESS
P O Box 7123
Berkeley, California 94707

Edited by C. Harris and M. Kuntz
Text Design by Hal Hershey
Cover Design by Fifth Street Design Associates

First printing, 1989

*Library of Congress Cataloging-in-Publication Data*

Miller, Arthur F.
    The truth about you.

    Reprint. Originally published: Old Tappan, N.J.:
F.H. Revell Co., ©1977.
    1. Success.  2. Self-perception.  3. Psychology,
Religious.  I. Mattson, Ralph.  II. Title.
BF637.S8M55      1987      158'.1      86-30159
ISBN 0-89815-194-5


Manufactured in the United States of America


1    2    3    4    5  —  93    92    91    90    89

# DEDICATION

*This edition is dedicated to*
Richard Bolles:

*conscience, midwife, and Joshua*
*to the career counseling profession.*

# Contents

# Acknowledgements

BERNARD HALDANE'S idea, expressed during the 1950's in his Success Factor Analysis (SFA), that individual excellence is reflected in achievement, was seminal to the System for Identifying Motivated Abilities (SIMA®) described in this book.

Others on our staff at People Management Incorporated have contributed to the technology of SIMA® through the thousands of hours spent in working with tens of hundreds of achievers and their managers. Most of the innovations have been reduced to usable format, procedures, or systems by Kim Miller. Early group training programs were built by Bob Andrews assisted by Jerry Haizlett, while John Paris pushed the rest of us towards greater complexity and sophistication in our report writing, and Jim Cunningham urged us toward simplicity.

In recent years, Rick Wellock has taught all of us how to help clients understand and make better use of their motivational patterns. Rob Stevenson has clarified the organization of data on people's strengths. Steve Darter has made our work much more useful in its search and counseling applications.

My sons Arthur and Kim have been the unheralded backbone of our analytical and casewriting capability, and are due special and continuing gratitude. Kit McDermott has been a most reliable staff case worker along with Rhonda LoBrutto.

Ralph Mattson joined us in 1979 and has contributed much in explanation of SIMA® and the work of PMI to church leaders and individual Christians. His has been a voice of unusual clarity and persuasion in helping people understand SIMA®.

By managing our business affairs so well, as Bob Gattorna has done, we are able to write books. For that I am most grateful. Persons within our greater "family" who have made special contributions include Marlys Hanson (Livermore), Dr. Nick Isbister (SIMA® UK), Tom Marshall (SIMA® Australasia), Ken Johnson (YWAM—Seattle), Rick Watring (Chicago).

Finally, I would like to mention my wife, Nancy Anne Miller, who has deepened my understanding about the implications of motivational patterns as explanation for so much of our internalized life as well as most of our behavior. And a special thank you to Constance Cather for all her typing and correcting and typing and correcting.

                                   Arthur F. Miller Jr.
                                   People Management Inc.
                                   10 Station Street
                                   Simsbury, CT 06070

# Introduction

MANY PEOPLE are uncertain about the rightness and usefulness of their lives. They are looking for signposts that will give them purpose and direction. In this book, a process is described that can change the life of any reader who is unsure of his or her direction. It provides a practical way to discover the "why?" of an unfulfilling career and to make sound decisions about the future. We hope that it will also help you see that you are gifted; that you have the means for deriving great enjoyment from a life of unique excellence and accomplishment.

Every person wants to lead a life that is both personally satisfying and valued by others. People want to make a difference—to count for something. They want to be "a somebody." They want to have a calling—a purpose of their lives. Unfortunately, many people are only vaguely aware of who they are and what they need to do to fulfill their longing.

Why don't more people lead richly satisfying lives and contribute handsomely to society? We believe that one reason is that the leaders of thought in this century collectively sold the notion that significance and satisfaction are byproducts of becoming somebody. You become somebody through a personal developmental process, or a manipulative, conditioning process, or a societal enculturating process. In other words, through some means, your putty is shaped, your blank slate is written on. You become you. In the contemporary version of "becoming," you transcend yourself without even knowing who you already are.

On the surface, becoming somebody seems parallel to the process of maturation, both biologically and psychologically. Young people navigate their youth and enter into adulthood assuming they will become somebody "when they grow up." So the emphases in their lives is the future, and they are sucked into all the educational and employment systems that seem to hold the promise of their future.

For example, you enter a process of education consuming up to 25% of your life expectancy, ostensibly in preparation for a productive and, hopefully, satisfying life and career. You, and your parents and their taxes and savings, enter into that system of education with the expectation that the educators know what they are doing. The fact is you enter into and complete a 12 to 20 year process without anyone at any time trying to find out what, how, or why you are motivated to learn. Even more distressing, no one in the educational world seems concerned about the fact that what you studied, how you were taught, and why you were expected to learn had little to do with how you were put together and what you ultimately did with your life or should have done with your life.

You enter the world of work. For one or several employers, over a period of 40 to 45 years, you are given assignments, coached, appraised, trained, developed, promoted, transferred, given results/objectives to fulfill, put in work groups, exhorted to make a commitment, expected to align with group goals outward bound exerorgies, rewarded, given additional incentives, sent for 3 months on an MBA program, ultimately retired into what for most is a waiting game bereft of personal significance, without anybody at any time during near half a century spending a few hours to find out what you are good at and motivated to do.

We believe that in America, the scenario of "becoming" has not provided the philosophy or means for a productive and satisfying life. Instead it has produced a cultural blindness where many of the bankers, managers, preachers, teachers, waitresses, mechanics, researchers, legislators, and architects do not belong in their trade; where stress is seen as endemic to work; where $800,000,000 is spent in one year to replace executives felled by circulatory disorders; where we excuse distracting and frequently destructive activities because we see them as necessary to provide meaning to life.

Through this book, we want to help reverse the tragic bondage our civilization suffers from because of a bankrupt understanding of human behavior. We hope to make a difference in how parents guide their youngsters, educators encourage learning, and employers select and manage their human resources. Most of all, we want to help people lead richly productive and satisfying lives.

All can be accomplished if you face the truth about you: You are designed to perform the works for which you are gifted. You have purpose. You have a calling. You have a destiny.

### ❧ *Part One* ❧

# A Call On Your Life

# CHAPTER ONE

# Who Do You Think You Are?

MOST OF US have gone through periods when we examine ourselves in mirrors in an attempt to understand who is hiding behind those eyes. After years of living with ourselves, we ask the same questions: Who am I? Why do I do what I do? What is my purpose? Where am I going?

Inane as these questions sometimes seem, they remain the material of profound art, philosophy, and theology. The issues are both incessant and inceptive: incessant because we continually strive to discover meaning beyond the apparent; inceptive because they trigger our thoughts to move in new directions. Most of us ask these questions because we yearn to discover joy by being who we should be. Hidden behind the practical problems we face is a longing to know how the joy we seek fits into who we are supposed to be and where our lives are going.

Who do you think you are? The question is simple but revolutionary because it suggests that the answer resides within *yourself* rather than in:

- What your family expects you to be.
- What your boss tries to make you.
- What your spouse wants you to be.
- What your teacher expects you to be.
- What your employees need you to be.
- What your friends tell you to be.
- What society wants you to become.

Most of us were brought up with the idea that we could *become* anything we wanted. From our earliest years, all options seemed open to us if we were willing to work hard enough. We could become doctors or potters or lawyers or teachers or carpenters or actors or artists or plumbers—anything we wanted. If we were willing to practice hard enough, we might even manufacture the talents we otherwise did not possess.

The world assumes you are something to mold or manipulate or shape or train or teach; that you are the raw material for someone else's intentions. For example, corporations believe it is possible to train people to become what is needed: a manager, a salesperson, or a planner. Schools believe that the pupils who are motivated to work for grades can be converted into students who learn for learning's sake. Churches believe that pastors who preach well but cannot administrate can be trained to develop into good administrators.

In reality, *people can be genuinely satisfied in their lives only when they attempt to develop what is in harmony with whoever they naturally are. Each of us has a unique design—a destiny.* Some people clearly manifest their destiny. From their earliest years, they fulfill a life design whether it involves inventing, composing, making money, painting, or politicking. Seeds of their eventual greatness are displayed so early that when fame comes, the destiny seems so obvious, the design so clear.

You may think having a destiny, romantic and attractive a concept as it is, has been reserved only for those who become famous. What is true of them is also true of you; you also have been designed. You also have a destiny.

Over the years, we have developed a process that can reveal your destiny in detail. Using this process, we have found that a behavior pattern emerged early in the life of every person we worked with. Relationships and achievements that were fulfilling for the person as a child were fulfilling for the adult, though on a higher level of sophistication. Increased experience, additional education, and maturing processes of all kinds were truly beneficial only when they enabled fulfillment of what the person always wanted to accomplish. In over 25 years of work, we have never seen an exception!

People are not only wonderfully and specifically designed, but this design remains consistent through life. This is not to say that there cannot be alterations in a person's life. Character and ethical values can change. Skills can be learned to increase effectiveness. Sloppy work habits or life-styles can be reorganized. All of these improvements enhance who we are but do not change our basic design. Who we start out to be matures, grows, and increases in understanding and power; but the design of the person to whom all this happens remains consistent.

# CHAPTER TWO

# Ignoring Who You Are Can Cost Your Life

THE NUMBER of people who have made crippling decisions about their educations or vocations is alarming. This suffering occurs because people do not know how they function and what gifts they possess. They believe life will be endowed with significance if they accept the values fostered by our educational and employment systems. Let us take a look at who some of these people are:

- Students whose majors have little relationship to their ultimate careers or even what they otherwise find meaningful in life.
- People who figuratively drop out of serious education while staying within the institutional walls because they are not studying subjects of interest to them.
- People who drop out of the educational process altogether because they cannot learn via standardized teaching methods.
- Workers who annually revolve through jobs as if jobs were turnstiles.
- Those persons in the teaching profession who are not motivated to teach.
- People who become supervisors or part of upper management who are not effective in those jobs.
- People who should never enter the people-helping professions, but do.
- People engaged in all fields who do not desire to do what they are being paid to do.

To say our society has an education and job mis-fit problem is like saying a full-blown hurricane is breezy. But in spite of the dire implications of this problem, our society remains blind to the fact that the systems of education and employment do not work for many individuals. *Most people educated and working within the American systems spend a significant part of their career in jobs for which they are poorly suited.*

In 1976, Dr. Herbert M. Greenberg, President of Marketing Survey and Research Corporation in Princeton, New Jersey, reported on a 16-year study that involved over 1,000 corporate clients and 350,000 persons. The study concluded that four out of five were in the wrong positions for their abilities. Daniel Yankelovitch, head of the public opinion research firm, Yankelovitch, Skelly, and White, Inc., reported in 1984 that only 13 percent of all Americans find their work truly meaningful. A 1987 survey of 6,000 professionals employed in a large multi-national corporation reported that about 70 percent did not believe their job made use of their talents.

Through our work with thousands of individuals over the past twenty-five years we've found that one-third of all managers do not belong in their positions. At least another third have serious problems with their jobs, since their abilities are not compatible with critical job requirements.

Among liberal arts college graduates, ample data demonstrate that *most students undertake studies unrelated to their abilities and the careers that they eventually enter.* In an effort to evaluate the direct utility of higher education in employment, the College Placement Council Foundation and the National Institute of Education sponsored the research of Bisconte and Solomon, who studied 12,000 graduates who had entered college in 1961. Among the findings of this study (*College Education on the Job: The Graduates Viewpoint*) are the following:

- Only 17 percent of the men and 31 percent of the women respondents had chosen their present careers before entering college. In fact, half of the women and nearly two-thirds of the men chose their present occupation after they completed their college education. Thus, while in college, the majority were not preparing specifically for their present work. For example, 38 percent ended up in business careers (business administration, sales, accounting, office work), although less than one in five majored in business.

- Only about one in four liberal education majors finds education very useful in imparting the knowledge and skills used in the present job.

- More surprising, perhaps, is that slightly more than half (56 percent) of the people currently employed as engineers find their college education very useful in providing knowledge they use in their present jobs.

Based on this kind of information, we believe that the wires of our education counseling machinery have been crossed—guidance counselors are not equipped with the necessary information about students to point them toward educational courses and careers commensurate with their capabilities and motivations. Instead the counselors unwittingly direct students into jobs that will not be fulfilling.

Because unsound guidance is the norm, we have a nation of unhappy employees; but not only are they unhappy, they become unhealthy. Job mis-fit kills. The stress and dissatisfaction associated with job mis-fit has been proven to shorten life.

In an impressive 15-year study of aging, the strongest predictor of longevity was *work satisfaction.* The second best predictor was overall "happiness." These two socio-physiological measures predicted longevity better than a rating by an examining physician of physical functioning, or a measure of the use of tobacco, or genetic inheritance. Controlling these other variables statistically did not alter the dominant role of *work satisfaction.* (U.S. Department of Health,

Education & Welfare, *Work in America: Report of a Special Task Force to the Secretary of Health, Education & Welfare*, MIT Press, 1973)

In addition to affecting the employee directly, the negative consequences of job mis-fit are multiplied because they also affect the families of unhappy employees. The results of a study examining job dissatisfaction among managers establish that it is a major cause of domestic problems.

> In studying the private and professional lives of more than 2,000 managers for nearly five years... after countless exchanges with managers and their wives and after careful analysis of research data, we concluded that the major determinant of work's impact on private life is whether negative emotional feelings aroused at work spill over into family and leisure time. When an executive experiences worry, tension, fear, doubt, or stress intensely, he is not able to shake these feelings when he goes home, and they render him psychologically unavailable for a rich private life. The manager who is unhappy in his work has a limited chance of being happy at home—no matter how little he travels, how much time he spends at home, or how frequently he takes a vacation.... When individuals feel competent and satisfied in their work—not simply contented, but challenged in the right measure by what they are doing—negative spillover does not exist. (Fernando Bartolome and Paul A. Lee Evans "Must Success Cost So Much?" *Harvard Business Review*, March-April 1980)

## THE IMPORTANCE OF INTRINSIC GIFTS

You may be questioning our concept of human design. Are we exaggerating the importance of intrinsic gifts? To answer this question, look at any city or town—each building, each telephone and computer; each book or work of visual art; each vehicle, tunnel, bridge and street; each garden; each tool; each marvelous cuisine; each dance and its music came from human gifts! Our civilization is only possible because millions of individuals exercise their talents and have done so through all of human history: from fire to the wheel to ice cream to 160 bushels of corn per acre to the Catscan to the Concorde and to genetic engineering.

With this picture in mind, we find it impossible to minimize the importance of human gifts. Excellence comes from the gifts of motivated individuals. Is it possible that radar was invented by someone who was not interested in electronics? Or that a person incompetent in structural engineering determined the stress parameters for buildings housing nuclear reactors? Or that a scrumptious apple pie was baked by someone who hated working in the kitchen? People who excel love what they do.

If civilization depends upon human gifts, the lack of interest in identifying and cultivating them is amazing. While a few others have developed similar ideas and conducted research that supports our findings, most professionals involved in "people research" are reluctant to accept our viewpoint. The reason for their hesitancy is not due to lack of evidence but because of their cultural assumptions. If researchers believe that people are putty and are to be shaped by social influences and training, then their basic assumption prevents the possibility of considering that humans already possess a complex design. The same holds true for those who begin with the premise that people are merely high-level animals rather than individuals with inherent differences. For researchers intent upon the "production" of human beings as dictated by the "needs" of society, the fact that individuals have an innate blueprint is an uncomfortable concept to entertain; it certainly puts a kink in their plans.

One of the problems we face in presenting our observations is that society has placed enormous confidence in psychology; psychologists being seen as the high-priests of the current age. Many people assume that psychologists' definitions are formulated with the objectivity used in the natural sciences. They think that the definitions of human beings provided by psychology are objectively true. What this means is that even if such definitions are *not* true, we become biased in our beliefs about ourselves. Biases can cripple us. They lead us away from the truth about ourselves, away from the self-knowledge necessary for making important life choices.

We feel that when considering careers, knowing an individual's personality or temperament is not necessary. What is vital is knowing what abilities—such as organizing, teaching, persuading, or analyzing—the job requires and whether the job candidate has those abilities. Psychology has influenced society to such an extent that we automatically find ourselves assessing people in psychological terms. By doing so, we overlook data on abilities; data required for dealing with career issues directly.

Do not make the mistake of assuming that one set of information can be extended to fit all circumstances. Information is situation dependent. Psychology has been useful in exploring problems in some areas of life; it has not been effective for predicting career fulfillment. For example, suppose you knew a man who could be described as lacking perseverance and relying heavily on his charm. With those two bits of information, a skilled clinical psychologist could delve deeper to help him face his problem. But this would not help the man gather data about his strengths, which would help him decide what career to pursue.

In our pursuit of self-knowledge, we often fail to distinguish between the kinds of information available to us. People use this wide variety of information ineffectively because they believe that facts are standardized—applicable to every situation. Over the last 20 years, experts within the field have increasingly acknowledged that scientific methodology is powerless to help understand the person as a unique individual.

These opinions indicate the emerging reaction in our society to psychology's failure to provide a science of persons. We suspect that increased awareness of our behavioral sciences' inadequacies may cause an overreaction. This could be in the form of a pseudo-mystical movement with tinges of parapsychology. In the past, principles of science have helped us be somewhat objective, but they may be impotent to stem the tide of irrational individuals, disheartened by psychology's failure, searching for an alternative method of assessing human behavior.

Psychology's primary focus has been pathology and the assessment tools developed to identify psychological flaws. Psychologists are experts at identifying what is wrong with people; yet we desperately need to find out what is *right* to encourage development.

We need to know our strengths.

We need to know the specifics about what motivates us, what abilities we possess, and where we can apply our gifts most effectively.

We need to know our design.

# CHAPTER THREE

# The Reunion

BEFORE WE introduce the process of self-understanding, let us pause and look at some everyday character types. We hope that by examining these characters, you will see the disparities between who people appear to be and who they would be if they followed their design. We will introduce these characters in the following vignette—the story of a reunion.

## THE CLASS OF '68

Being dragged to her parents' 20-year class reunion was not all bad for Jenny; it gave her the opportunity to write an editorial for her high school paper on what people of the class of '68 were doing with their lives. The discussions she heard while waiting on tables and serving refreshments provided a lot of material. Her reluctance about giving up a Saturday gave way to curiosity, astonishment, and then compassion as she realized how many disasters, how much pain, and how little success was being relived in this compressed weekend.

During breaks, Jenny scribbled down snatches of gossip and confessions. Early on she gave each person a label to capture their unique behavior. Later, when she went to write her column, she grouped each person into one of three categories: The successes, the failures, and the ones in between success and failure. Considering the promise for success demonstrated by many of the individuals during high school the results 20 years later were often surprising. Here is a sample of what she found:

### The "Successes"

ENTREPRENEUR: Though he almost flunked out of school and did not go to college, he always had a money-making scheme on the side. At 38, he owns several businesses, has made and lost a fortune, and is on the verge of going public with a new business of which he is one-third owner.

POLITICIAN: She literally ran the school, had her feet in all the camps (swingers, jocks, intellectuals, and nerds), and was even respected by the faculty. She was elected to the state house of representatives four years after finishing law school and is about to run for state treasurer.

OLD RELIABLE: He was always responsible because he would do anything asked of him, he was one of the spear carriers in the operetta, Spanish Club treasurer, and the football team's water boy. Now he's a prosperous banker in a nearby inner-city institution.

DIFFERENT DRUMMER: Of all the success stories, her success was the biggest surprise. No one remembered her name from school because she was an outcast. But she recently received a $50,000 award from an international meteorological commission for discovering a method to forecast drought cycles.

## The "Failures"

BRAIN: In high school, he surpassed others in every subject, went on to get bachelors' degrees in English, economics, and history and a master's in anthropology. But he has been delivering mail for the last 10 years.

STAR: She was the pretty girl who had the lead in all the plays, could sing and dance, and had a good figure. At 19 she married a good-looking jock who worked in a vocational trade. They raised four kids. At the reunion, looking much older than her age, she seemed defeated and dejected.

PERSONALITY: He was the most popular boy in the high school class, but he studied little, and did not complete college. He began a career in sales, had been with many companies, and had just lost another job.

DAREDEVIL: He was known during high school for doing outrageous stunts on his bike. After graduation, he continued to take hair-raising risks, becoming involved in an insurrection in the Middle East. In addition, he had been arrested several times for possession of drugs. His life was as directionless as it had been 20 years ago.

RENAISSANCE MAN: The class's answer to superman. In addition to being gifted in tennis, wrestling, chess, and madrigals choir, he was handsome and sensitive, an honor roll student, and a nut about Shakespeare and abstract expressionism. Yet, career and home life had been a series of starts and stops; he couldn't settle into a career or a geographical location.

## The Ones "In Between"

CRUSADER: She led the campaign against the dress code, the Vietnam War, and the use of pesticides in the gypsy moth invasion. Her career with an advertising firm left her terribly tired and angry.

HOT DOG: In high school, she was the popular rich girl: the cheerleader, the classy dresser, the sports car driver. She could always get others to do her homework. She didn't go to college and went through two marriages. Last year she was promoted from her position as receptionist and entered a junior college's evening program for working adults.

COUNSELOR: Everybody went to him when they were in trouble or in need of a shoulder. He did okay in school, went to college, got his master's in psychology, and is working for a manufacturing firm in the Midwest, administering an employee assistance program.

Jenny became depressed as she realized how a lack of self-knowledge could result in meaningless and irresponsible lives. She wondered if the members of her class would also be unfulfilled in 20 years. She interviewed her classmates who resembled the "characters" from the previous generation to see if they knew who they were or what they wanted from life. Most did not, and Jenny knew that she was part of this majority. She had started to visit colleges, knowing her education would cost $50,000 and require four years of her life, yet she couldn't decide what she should study. Jenny knew she liked to write when inspired and she found it easy. She liked people. She liked to see her name in print. Should she pursue a career in journalism?

Jenny had no easy answer for herself or one for her classmates. She closed her article with forced encouragement, telling the readers to set goals for their educations and careers.

## THE SEARCHERS: JOSH

Also conscripted by his parents to serve at their reunion weekend activities, Jenny's brother spent his time refereeing volleyball on the beach, and serving as lifeguard for the alumni and their kids. Inquisitive by nature, Josh introduced himself to the participants and asked them what they did and solicited advice about what kind of college major he should select. As a sophomore he had struggled to survive this far without making a commitment and was now being asked to make an educational decision of consequence. He enjoyed the fraternity, the girls, and being on the junior varsity football and soccer teams but in his classes, he found college all he had feared it would be. Academics were never his cup of tea. But what to do?

Unfortunately, his conversations were with those alumni who had never gotten their act together. He later shared some of these experiences with Jenny and they both realized he had talked with STAR, DAREDEVIL, and HOT DOG.

Jenny and Josh realized the risk involved with the decisions they faced after overhearing the alumni. They went to their parents for some answers and discovered they were talking to PIONEER and SCOREKEEPER.

PIONEER had enjoyed a richly satisfying career in laser research for over 10 years. Several years ago when funding for his specialty dried up he accepted a promotion and became department head of technical services. As a result of changing positions, he has been undergoing a career crisis. He told his children that he had loved to invent and with that aspect of his work missing, he found his job unfulfilling. His only advice was to make career changes while they were young if they weren't happy.

SCOREKEEPER was more helpful. She believed people could find the right occupation if they were true to their feelings. Motherhood had only partially fulfilled her so when Jenny was five, SCOREKEEPER began keeping the books for small companies. She enjoyed the work and her business thrived. She felt that working on a personal computer from home provided the flexibility she required of a career. She advised her kids to keep a diary for six months, listing activities they liked and those they disliked. Then they should look for patterns.

## BECOMING A SUCCESS

Your opportunity for success and satisfaction in school and/or in your career requires that the work engages both your *talents* and your *motivations*. The untapped potential of many of the alumni in the reunion story was the result of failing to match their work to their strengths. Those who succeeded did so either by luck or by consistently following an intuitive sense of what was right for them.

Because of our years of working with people and how they function when they are doing what they are good at and are motivated to do, we can make fairly reliable guesses about the reasons for success or failure in the lives of the class of '68 characters.

ENTREPRENEUR didn't do well in school because the educational reward system held little importance for him. Besides, he learns by doing. Only when motivated by the opportunities and pay-off involved in starting a new business did he take off. He made some mistakes, but he earned a lot of money in the learning process and had a "blast."

POLITICIAN began her apprenticeship during high school. In her state government job, she continues to use skills that she demonstrated she possessed while in student government positions.

OLD RELIABLE got his name by meeting others' needs. He majored in accounting because he was good with numbers. After college, he began working in the inner city to provide financial services for families.

DIFFERENT DRUMMER followed her love of learning to the top; she earned a doctorate in probability theory and did postdoctoral research on weather forecasting systems. She now works for the government in agricultural research. She remained true to herself though her walk was sometimes lonely.

On the other hand, those who were in positions that didn't hold their interest did not fare so well.

BRAIN loved the stimulation involved in learning. He found working as a postal carrier tedious but it paid for his career as a student. He feared settling into more challenging work. He was convinced all jobs would be stifling after six months and that he'd be obligated to remain with a company that had spent the time and money to train him.

STAR needed visibility but assumed that was a fault. She married young, had children, and suppressed her desire to be recognized for roles in addition to those of wife and mother. After the fourth child was born, she convinced herself that she was fated to be unfulfilled.

PERSONALITY didn't learn to work hard early in life because he didn't need to. Everyone yielded to his charm. Later, when expected to produce and be held accountable for his sales, he would quit and look for companies with lower expectations.

DAREDEVIL discovered that nobody would pay him to leap high buildings. He was addicted to the thrills and didn't understand how to integrate that characteristic into a viable career.

RENAISSANCE MAN never realized that diverse skills could be integrated into a single role: a generalist. After demonstrating certain proficiency in jobs with a narrow focus, his boredom prompted him to move on.

CRUSADER sold out; she settled for a job that didn't demand her drive and abilities. Her work in advertising paid well but didn't fulfill her need to affect some change. She didn't realize that governmental, religious, and educational agencies needed her talent.

HOT DOG is on the path to a meaningful career but needs to pay the dues required for a trade or profession.

COUNSELOR would excel in the employee assistance program if he changed roles. He is motivated when interacting directly with people in need. His administration duties keep him at arms length from those he wants to help.

Each of these characters failed to recognize what kind of work would engage them. But such recognition first requires that people understand who they are. Not knowing enough about oneself to enter and stay in an appropriate career is not confined to our reunion characters. The problem is experienced by most people for too much of their lives.

In this next chapter we will discuss methods that people have used to gain self-knowledge. But first we would like you to examine your own situation. Ask yourself these questions as a warm-up for getting to know yourself.

1. How much of your formal education has been useful in your occupation?

   A. more than 50%
   B. less than 50%
   C. less than 25%

2. How much of your formal education has been useful in areas of your life other than your vocation?

   A. more than 50%
   B. less than 50%
   C. less than 25%

3. Of all the teachers you have had, how many really inspired you?

   A. more than 10
   B. between 5 and 10
   C. less than 5

4. How much of your job engages what you have to offer?

   A. more than 50%
   B. less than 50%
   C. less than 25%

5. How many of your jobs have made substantial use of your talents?

   A. more than 3
   B. 1 or 2
   C. none

Most people with whom we have worked answered "C" for each question. They did not know enough about themselves to choose the appropriate education and jobs.

Self-knowledge is a prerequisite to a fulfilling life. The question you may be asking is: *How do I find out who I am, what I have to offer, and what I want out of life?* Parts II and III of the book will help you answer those questions.

## Part Two

# Finding Your Destiny

CHAPTER FOUR

# Will You Climb the Mountain?

SINCE WE ARE about to launch you into a considerable effort to discover your design, and we don't want you to flinch but dive right in, we thought we might review some of the rationale and reasons for urging you to try.

Most of us have heard people say "He is not motivated," or "She has no motivation." In response, we may think of an uncommitted, lazy, individual who has no desire to succeed. Parents, supervisors, and teachers can offer convincing evidence that someone is not motivated by pointing out a failure on this person's part to perform a required task; but you should not conclude that this means an absence of motivation. Some people appear unmotivated because of the irrelevance of their motivation to their current job. Others were raised in families in which achievement was not encouraged. The truth is that everyone is motivated. Everyone has certain abilities he or she is motivated to use, certain abilities he or she is not motivated to use, and many aptitudes he or she is neither good at, or motivated to use. By nature, people are motivated by a specific combination of what the outcome of their actions are, why they want that outcome, and how they can best achieve that particular outcome. These motivations are apparent only when we watch a person performing a task of their own choosing. We call the abilities used to perform these tasks *motivated abilities*.

## MOTIVATIONAL PATTERNS

As we have said previously, discoveries about motivated abilities did not originate in theory but through our observations of people made during 25 years of counseling. The phenomenon of motivated abilities was confirmed in every case. In addition, we found that the way an individual uses his or her motivated abilities remains consistent over that person's lifetime. Among the wide variety of activities in which an individual participates, a consistent pattern of behavior can be identified. We call the individual's consistent use of his or her motivated abilities a *motivational pattern*. Just as people are sure to have hearts, finger-prints, and ears, the nature of human beings ensures that each of us has a design or motivational pattern that emerges in childhood and stays consistent through-out our lives. In some cases, this pattern is easy to identify; in others it is more complex. However, in all lives it is distinctive, and many of our clients have exclaimed, "Of course, that's how I always operate. That's exactly right. Why didn't I know this all along!"

We have been in an ideal position to observe the phenomenon of *individual* human design and have reacted to our findings with delight. The realization that each of us can discover our pattern grants us freedom; we can stop feeling guilty for not trying to become someone else and can move confidently in directions that reflect who we are naturally.

What have people learned about themselves by knowing their motivational patterns? The following are a few examples:

- *Conviction of self-worth*: Most people realize immediately that they are worthwhile and have something of value to offer.

- *Explanation of the past:* An individual can evaluate why certain job situations, roles, and relationships have failed or succeeded.

- *Clarification of direction:* A motivational pattern clarifies the path one's life should take. If headed the wrong way, an individual has a reliable compass against which he or she can correct the direction.

- *Understanding reasons for behavior:* Individuals gain insight regarding the details of why they function as they do. People see their whole system of behavior: how they perceive and approach work, what they emphasize or diminish, who they move toward or stay away from, why they are responsive to certain assignments and avoid others, which kinds of problems they attack and which they leave unsolved, what makes them angry or frustrated or depressed or excited, why they function the way they do in a social situation.

## SPECIFIC APPLICATIONS

Even a superficial understanding of motivational patterns clarifies much about a person's needs. In many situations, thorough understanding can be used to great advantage. The following are a few specific ways motivational patterns can be used:

### In High Schools and Colleges

- To help teenagers make educational and vocational decisions.
- To help teachers determine what and how each student will learn.
- To give schools a method for selecting motivated teachers.
- To help college students identify a professor's characteristic patterns of thinking so questions can be framed to most effectively draw out information.

Help college students identify the types of work, boss, organization, condition, and goals they will find motivating.

## *Interpersonal Relationships*

- To help couples considering marriage see the inherent dynamics in their relationship and be aware and prepared for the types of conflicts most likely to arise.
- To help couples build their relationship according to their patterns and prevent conflict in decisions.
- To give parents a practical system for understanding and guiding their children.

## *In the Work Place*

- To help managers select suitable employees, build the organization on complementary strengths, and redistribute tasks to fully engage employees' available talents.
- To give employees a method to evaluate their current positions and to increase their job satisfaction.
- To help organizations find reasons for poor employee performance and either improve job fit or build coping strategies.
- To give unemployed persons a procedure to define, locate, and land the right job.

You may wonder if we overestimate the usefulness of motivational patterns; however, we feel their fundamental nature lends itself to many and diverse applications. Whenever people are involved, so are their motivated intentions, whatever interests individuals also engages their motivated abilities.

To fulfill your potential, you must build your life around your gifts. Your work, leisure activities, community involvement, relationships, and expressions of faith should require your gifts. Then your promise will be demonstrated.

## TAKING TIME TO FIND YOUR PATTERN

You cannot depend on others to identify your motivational pattern and you may already have paid dearly by not knowing. Though much is to be gained by your family, your employer and society if your gifts are discovered, you yourself must take the time to understand your motivational pattern. You are responsible for putting your gifts into action. When your gifts are carefully nurtured through education or apprenticeship and then used in a responsible way, the results are wonderful to watch and satisfying to deliver.

Many people believe that people belong to one of two classes: the "gifted" or the "average." The gifted are the visibly successful people; those whose abilities are recognizably superior. The average are those who wish they were gifted. In any area, some people have outstanding abilities and are recognized for them. A small number possess the natural brilliance that almost automatically leads to fame. Others, such as entertainers, have gifts that are highly visible and are rewarded extravagantly. But these exceptions should not blind you to the realization that everyone is gifted.

The fact that each of us cannot be famous is not a tragedy; only certain people are built for fame. Nor should the knowledge that we all cannot be leaders be demoralizing; most of us are not interested. As we have said before, contentment does not come from being a celebrity or making lots of money for work that you do not love. Nor is it the result of making peace with mediocrity. Contentment comes from identifying the gifts you have been given, submitting them to the necessary training, and then engaging them in work. If used appropriately, your gifts provide material and personal rewards for you and your employer.

Few people have achieved success without relying on their gifts. Successful services and products are the direct result of individuals using what they have been given. People need encouragement to use their gifts. No successful person was "self-made;" successful people are those smart enough or grateful enough to be good stewards of their gifts.

Have you ever paused to watch a waitress well suited for her work serving a table of hungry customers? Notice how well she deflects their impatience; how she anticipates requests; how pleasantly she replaces an overdone steak; how she keeps an eye on her tables as she makes her rounds. Compare her performance with the more common experience of being served by someone who does not have the required gifts.

Do you recall a teacher who lit up a subject for you? Remember how they made complicated problems seem simple; how they showed concern; how they joked and stormed and grew serious in the same class hour! Contrast their class with other classes that were taught by individuals whose gifts did not foster learning.

People gifted at their work are a pleasure to watch. A shoemaker manipulating a fine piece of leather, a parent alternately disciplining and consoling a child, a repairman tracking down the problem, an internist diagnosing an illness, an errorless typist beating the deadline, a cabinetmaker designing an updated kitchen, an executive secretary effectively handling difficult clients, a singer juggling the octaves, a writer bringing life to the page, a minister inspiring a congregation, an artist catching vision on canvas, a coach inspiring a discouraged team, a comic helping people take themselves less seriously, a surgeon, toolmaker, and dentist deftly working with their hands. We have all observed the phenomenon of motivational patterns at work in other people. Now we must look inward and recognize the abilities within ourselves. *That is the lesson.*

Can you imagine how your life would improve if you were aware of your motivational pattern and could put it to full use? Can you imagine how society would benefit if people were educated and employed on the basis of their gifts?

# CHAPTER FIVE

# Where To Look

YOU HAVE in your memory all the data you will need to discover your own design. The process we are going to describe to help you find your design does not require psychological introspection; the information you will evaluate is not the mysterious behavior of a hidden self. Most people enjoy this self-examination process because to collect the necessary data, you deal with only positive behavior.

## SIGNS OF YOUR DESIGN

Signs of your design appeared early in life. Certain activities from childhood stand out in your memory; why do they emerge so easily while most other memories dim? Because these vivid childhood memories are very likely early signs of your design, your motivational pattern. Going through your personal history, you will find a host of events that were meaningful although you may not be able to explain why. For example, you may have memories of activities such as the following:

- Winning all the marbles.
- Organizing all the junk in the basement.
- A knack for drawing animals.
- Exploring the woods.
- Enlisting in contests.
- Being lead in junior play.
- An inclination to "go it alone."
- Experimenting with explosives.
- Building a soap box racer.
- Paint-by-the numbers prize.
- Contribution to camp cooking.
- Improvising a pair of cross-country skis.

Your memories might appear to be a collection of unrelated or inconsequential events, but they are not haphazard; they *are* evidence of your design.

## EXAMINING THE WILL

The influences of parents and peers, emotional and psychological factors, impulses, requirements of physical and economic survival, job demands, even indigestion have a great impact on our intentions. How do you separate the actions that express *who you are* from all the internal and external reactions that have little to do with your design? The answer to this question requires an understanding of the will.

Try to imagine the will having a shape that is as unique from individual to individual as are physical characteristics. Though we're discussing the spiritual component of humans, which obviously cannot be seen, the will can be said to manifest a spiritual shape through its intentions. Each person's will has unique shape so each motivational pattern—the way in which the will expresses itself—is unique.

People *do* things. The way a person does them, and what he or she intends to accomplish, is not caused by chance. The will is the individual's core, affecting intentions, attitudes, and behavior. Actions that originate in a particular will form a motivational pattern because of their consistency. When you examine what a person freely wills to do, you will find embedded in his or her actions a unique, consistent pattern expressive of that person's intentions. Reactions to another's will or to environmental or survival needs impede the ability to perceive motivational patterns. To avoid such complications, you should examine only the actions that resulted in your personal satisfaction—ones that when recalled years later, bring back some of the satisfaction you felt at the time.

In our experience, the accomplishments that reveal the unique way in which you are designed always have the following elements:

- The achievement activities resulted in a feeling of joy or satisfaction, regardless of their significance in others eyes.

- The person felt the achievement activities were done well, regardless of what other people thought.

Let us examine these elements more carefully. Note that we use the phrase *achievement activities* and not the word *successes*. In our culture success is equated with becoming upwardly mobile: famous or rich. While wealth and notoriety can be considered necessary aspects of achievement activities for some people, the outcome of achievement activities does not necessitate success as society generally views it. Not everyone has a series of successes to remember; few of us have been chosen as captain of the team, elected to political office, the recipient of awards and job promotions. We cannot all win society's recognition for our achievement activities.

Because our culture is preoccupied with moving up, each of us must fight the tendency to judge ourselves according to this scale. We must create individual definitions of success. Longing for audiences and applause when they have little relationship to your gifts is useless. Working in an organization at a level above the one where you function best is to deny yourself contentment. When you long for gifts other than those you possess you diminish your uniqueness and potential for joy. Participating in activities outside your range of abilities prevents the pleasure of experiencing and demonstrating competence.

Don't allow the world to press you into a mold. Ignore the pressure to become what others want you to become. Discover who you are. Participate in the wonder of being unique.

# CHAPTER SIX

# Gathering The Right Data

IN THE PAST few decades techniques for obtaining self-knowledge have become popular. Some, rooted in Eastern religion, are steeped in mysticism. Others are based on theories and the validity of the results cannot always be demonstrated. Often, following the procedures for these techniques is complex; and once completed, results apply only to personal life and are irrelevant elsewhere. The technique for finding motivational patterns is easy to comprehend; the results come from a person's achievement activities.

We are working with a universal phenomenon. A pattern has become apparent from the achievement activities of every person we have evaluated and yours will too. Do not worry that you may not have a motivational pattern; having a pattern is a guaranteed ingredient in humans.

## NOT ANY DATA—THE RIGHT DATA

Without guidance regarding the type of information that should be gathered when examining the past for achievement activities, a person can easily fall into the trap of collecting data that will lead the person no closer to identifying his or her motivational pattern. You should not look for *milestones*. Some people review their past and see when they became an Eagle scout, when they graduated from high school, whey they were married, when they received their master's degree, and when they had their first child. In some cases, these events can be considered achievement activities; but in general this is not the kind of data required.

Another data error is the chronology of personal history. For example, "I got my first job in 1958; got my degree in 1963; divorced in 1972; built our present home within 2 years of 2nd marriage." Chronology has a role in the life of an individual but is a hindrance in identifying one's design.

A third error is to assume that the events that had *psychological significance* are achievement activities. "When I realized that I didn't love my husband..." Since many of these events involve trauma and reactions to other people and circumstances, such data normally don't reveal giftedness.

A crucial difference between achievement data and these other kinds of information is that *achievement activities selected by the subject are efforts involving both abilities and motivations*. The only criteria the activity must meet is that you enjoyed the activity and felt you did it well (for the age you did it).

Other data (e.g. milestones, personal chronology, psychologically significant) do not reveal motivated behavior.

One of the delights of speaking to audiences about motivational patterns is that many people have noticed consistency in their own behavior or that of family members and can recognize that what we are saying is true. They did not know how to describe the elements of these patterns, but they have seen them in action. Here are some examples:

A mother of two sons always wondered why one of them was highly organized while the other had to be reminded repeatedly that his clothes should be in the hamper or his closet, not piled in the corner and under his bed. She knows her children have had the same parents, the same instruction, environment, and discipline; she also has evidence that they did not turn out the same.

A college student who has attempted to stick to a rigorous study schedule since she was in high school still finds herself procrastinating. As deadlines approach, she works quickly and effectively to complete the assignment or project. In contrast, her roommate proceeds methodically, the way instructors claim it should be done. The student has evidence that she will never be like her roommate and has concluded that she doesn't have to be.

A personnel trainer in a large corporation who has spent years attempting to turn non-managers into managers and people weak in sales into winning salespersons knows that different people are capable of different things.

The individuals in these examples are basing their opinions on observations. However, each of these individuals has come to realize the wisdom of working with what is already given instead of attempting to make the person into a different person.

When understood, a person's behavior becomes a resource from which conclusions with lifelong implications can be drawn. We encountered a splendid example of the acceptance of motivational patterns in *Painting Techniques of the Masters* by Hereward Leseter Cooke (Watson-Guptill, 1972). He writes that following intuition will lead you to the details of how to practice your art; instinct will reveal how to express yourself. Addressing the apprentice on the subjects of color, style, subject matter, and artistic convictions, he advised the following:

(On Color) One thing you must do early in your career is to find out *what color harmonies come naturally to you*. No two painters have the same sense of color harmonies, and it is very important that you *find where your instincts lie* ... The history of art proves that the great masters—with only a few exceptions—found and kept to a rather narrow color range during most of their active careers.

(On Style) One of the most difficult and important things you will ever have to do is to decide just what kind of a painter you want to be. *No two people react in the same way* to the world around them . . . This is an invariable rule of art history; only when a painter is painting what appeals to him, *in a way that appeals to him*, is there a chance of producing a worthwhile picture.

(On Subject Matter) Next, decide what subject *you would really like to paint* if you had a free choice. Some people are naturally drawn to landscapes, others to flowers, abstract shapes, birds, machines, portraits, nudes, the range of subjects is almost infinite. Again, *be honest with yourself.* You will never be able to alter your *instinctive preferences* . . . for an artist, the road to hell is paved with pictures which are not sincerely felt.

(On Convictions) Having made up your mind about the subject and the style, *follow your convictions*. If you really feel a preference for Corot's landscapes, for example, don't let anyone tell you it is out of date, and if you *follow your convictions* without deviation, the world eventually will beat a path to your doorstep . . . Therefore, have the *courage of your convictions* and *paint what and how you like*."

Cooke had marvelous insight to know that each artist's talent finds its ultimate expression when true to itself.

You may accept the validity of motivational patterns for those who lead, create, or burn with the crusader's heart but you may have difficulty believing this principle can be applied to anyone. But when you see a person doing something well, the harmony between his or her motivational pattern and the job or role or form of expression is apparent. Careers and tasks when well suited to the individual's gifts are finely honed expressions of that person's design. If we are true to our design, we can move into the right career and find the exact achievement activities to express our unique intentions.

By identifying achievement activities from your earliest memories to the present, you can describe your motivational pattern in detail. Most people are unaware of the resource they have available within themselves to help make sensible life choices. Recurring behavior patterns can tell you much about your design. Instead of fighting the tendencies of how you operate, examine them and then put them to work for you.

Before you gather your own data you may find it helpful to examine the achievement activities of someone else to see the evidence for a pattern. Because the motivational pattern emerges early in life and remains consistent, achievements listed begin in childhood and extend through adulthood. This chronological listing is helpful in the recollection process because there is a naturalness and easy flow about it. It, however, is not essential. You may prefer a more random recollection, or to start with the present and work backward.

The italicized statements in the following case study are from a list written by the achiever. The words following them are edited quotes from a taped interview in which the achiever elaborated on how she accomplished her achievements.

## LISTING THE DATA: AN EXAMPLE

### Childhood

*Fixing up a crow's wing. Taking care of the bird for about a week and letting him go when he was well.*

I guess I was seven or eight—I was always collecting animals. One day I walked into this crow—I guess it had a broken wing. I really wasn't sure—but it couldn't take off, so I carried it upstairs. Had a bird cage. Put the crow in there. So I took care of him. Then after about a week or so, we just opened the little door and let the bird find its wings.

### Teen Years

*Working with my animals.*

Had a cow, good old Elsie. She developed mastitis. Poor Elsie was a pretty good producer but not the best. My father wanted to sell her. I objected—I violently objected. She was one of my cows. I called the vet and he came out. He gave her some shots—made her a sack out of a rubber apron—hung it over her back. I worked with this cow three days straight. The mastitis stopped and never came back again—she became one of our best producers.

### Age 22-25

*Became officer in U.S. Navy; received exceptional and outstanding fitness reports.*

I took over a pretty much run-down education-and-information office and built it up to the point where everybody knew about it. When I walked in there it was a mess. Got rid of a couple of people—had them transferred out. Built up a library—wrote instructions as to what to expect people to do before they go up for their examinations.

### Age 26-30

*Managed a singing group on "off-duty time." They won the District Talent Show and were sent to New York (lost up there.)*

Started talking over a radio station. Had my own program—base radio—had a program of classical music. Looked in the other room and there were four sailors harmonizing, so I started listening to them. They were not bad—they were going to sing someplace and then I found out they didn't make it because they got confused as to where it was. So I said, "You need a manager." We started out with the base club. About a year later we had covered 55 performances in the area—won the first prize in Charlotte. Then we got guitars organized and went up to Goshen—won there.

(We want to point out that some of you were absorbed in reading about this individual's achievements, while others found it tedious. Your own motivational pattern was in operation, even during this exercise. Some readers do not need encouragement to examine personal details because they are motivated to enjoy it.)

## REVIEWING THE DATA

The next step in identifying the motivational pattern is to review the case, looking for repetitive elements and determine the pattern. To help you do this, think about the answers to these key questions.

1. How would you describe the way the person wants to relate to or operate with others *(as part of a team? As the boss? As an individualist)*?

2. What abilities does the person manifest in the achievements *(organizing, debating, overseeing)*?

3. What objects or subject matter does the person want to work with *(numbers, things, people, ideas, words)*?

4. What end result or payoff does the person gain from the achievements *(excelling, building and developing, acquiring things, gaining a response)*?

Though the individual in the example filled 13 pages with her achievements, you need only the material presented previously to answer the questions and to reach the more obvious conclusions about her motivational pattern. After you finish, check them against our findings listed below.

1. Motivated to be the boss, to run things and people, to control and direct others.

2. Motivated to develop, to persuade, and to advocate.

3. Motivated to work with people (and animals).

4. Motivated to gain a response from others and to influence their behavior.

Now that you have had a taste of what achievement activities are and how to identify some of the ingredients of motivational patterns, which will be covered in more detail in Chapter 8. We shall get you started in the fascinating experience of recalling your own satisfying achievements to see what they say about you.

# CHAPTER SEVEN

# Recalling The Good Times

THE FIRST STEP in the identification of your motivational pattern is to recall and describe your achievement activities. All conclusions about your motivational pattern are based on historical evidence. We call the process used for gathering your achievement information a SIMA interview. SIMA stands for System for Identifying Motivated Abilities. The steps of the system include the completion of a SIMA Biographical Information Form (included in Appendix A), the SIMA interview itself and finally, an analysis of the data. The end result is a description of your motivational pattern.

In the process of completing a SIMA interview you discover information that reveals your strengths, which is why we ask you to recall only the activities that you felt you were good at and found satisfying. All of us need to cope with disappointing life experiences to mature. However, motivated abilities cannot be identified by examining the negative experiences. Also, you should avoid events that were experiences only and not something you *did* or *accomplished*.

## THE SIMA INTERVIEW

Because most people talk more readily than they write, the SIMA interview is easy to do. We suggest you enlist a helpful friend, inquisitive ally, mentor, or counselor to listen as you describe *how* you accomplished your achievement activities. Approach this in a way that feels comfortable to you. If instead of a one-on-one interview, you prefer a small group, gather several of your friends and do the exercise together. If you normally talk to your golden retriever or to yourself, that's fine too.

Whoever you choose, make sure the interview is documented. We recommend recording it on audio tape but a third person could take notes if that's more convenient. We also suggest that your interviewer study your completed Biographical Form, and the following interview procedures. Familiarity with the procedures improves the interviewer's ability to draw out the details of your achievement activities.

### Instructions for the Interviewer

A SIMA interview helps obtain a more complete report of someone's achievement activities. To conduct an interview, simply read the interviewee's Biographical Information Form, starting with the earliest achievements and working to the present. The purpose of the interview is for the individual to expand on his other experiences.

In a SIMA interview, you are after *the mechanics* or *details* of an achievement: a step-by-step account of the person's actions and what he or she enjoyed about them. As the interviewee talks, you tape what is said or a third person can take notes. Though the process is relatively simple you'll obtain a more accurate report of the achievements if you take the following precautions.

- *Avoid leading questions.* Do not explore areas the interviewee has not opened.

- *Avoid leading questions.* Do not explore areas because they are of personal interest to you.

- *Avoid leading questions.* If the interviewee is currently being considered for employment, do not explore areas critical to that position.

- *Don't conduct the interview by any other rules.* In a SIMA interview, you do not have a two-way flow of communication; you do not try to win the interviewee's confidence through technique, manner, or other method; you do not try to give or receive impressions; you do not play a role.

- *Avoid judging.* All people desire to fulfill their motivations. Someone's achievement activities may appear selfish or selfless, but all individuals seek personal satisfaction.

To begin the interview read the description of the first chronological achievement activity and interviewee you ask to "tell you about the details of what he or she did." Focus on the achievement until you have gotten all the details the interviewee can recall. It might help to use questions such as these:

- Would you give me more details of what you did?
- Give me an illustration of what you mean by ...?
- Would you give me one example of that?
- What was your role?
- What were you good at?
- How did you accomplish that aspect?
- Could you tell me about that?
- What did you enjoy about that?

If you are taking notes rather than taping the interview, you should also do the following:

- Note any details that describe what was actually done.

- Note, verbatim if possible, words that reveal: an ability *organized, sold*; a subject matter worked with—*machines*; *figures* the nature of the interactions with others—*did it all by myself*; what was enjoyed—*I won*; *he gave me $10.*

- When an illustration is given, note those features the achiever emphasized—*first order from P&B—took a year to do—nobody suggested— sold Chief Engineer first.*

- Take down quotes verbatim—*"Teacher said, 'Helen, you're incredible.'"*

- Note any numbers used—*made $38.47 my first day*

### Interviewing Procedure for the Interviewee

You should talk for 10 to 15 minutes on each achievement. Remember

- to give detailed examples for items that were only generalized about on the Biographical Information. Expand on statements such as *I used to do a lot of 4-H projects* or *I made some very tough sales* or *I used to coordinate a lot of affairs.*

- to give details of how you *organized, built, persuaded, solved problems.*

- to give details of your process for an activity that can be done in various ways: playing tennis, football, or chess; sewing a dress; building a tree house; raising a cow; or training a child.

- to explain how you became involved in the achievements activity.

- to discuss your role if it was a group activity and explain what you did.

-  to describe in detail the objects you worked with: a school newspaper, a soap box derby car, hospital patient, a room design, or a new product. Discuss each object's complexity, your involvement with it, and other data that reveal the type of subject matter with which you like to work.

Studying the following examples may help you during the interview process. Again, the italicized statements are taken from a Biographical Information Form, and the extended descriptions of the achievement activities are edited quotes from the interview.

*Planted a patch of cucumbers; maintained, harvested and sold crop—reinvesting part of the profits for several years in future crops.*

When it came time to harvest, was taken to where they sorted the cucumbers out. Got the checks back in my name—paid back for the seed—put some of the money away. One-quarter acre—had to hoe them and keep them clean. Had to be sure you pick them on time, they get too big. Had to have a little judgment on when to pick them, what size to pick. I really enjoyed the money and the fact that I was making money—that I could produce something. Nice to look at the field and see it nice and clean—fun to plant something and watch it grow.

*Writing, casting, directing and starring in a senior class commencement night skit.*

Remember more about that, I think, than anything else in school—putting together a kind of take off on the last scene from Hamlet where everybody gets killed. Enjoyed reading Shakespeare. Wrote rhyming couplets—enough to fill in 20 minutes to half an hour on stage. Got casting from people I knew in the class—got the son of the principal. Directed rehearsals. Ran through the parts, got them to memorize the roles, all without faculty assistance. It was the hit of the particular occasion. My drama teacher insisted that I had not written the thing. It gave me great pleasure—I enjoyed the performing aspect and the directing, putting it all together. Had many aspects to it. It was a situation I felt a lot of confidence about. I knew what I wanted to do. I was in the thick of it all—driving it, participating it, getting some good reactions and vibrations.

A final note: When people describe non-motivated behavior, they usually talk *about* the subject. When they describe motivated behavior, it becomes a lively narration of how they accomplished the tasks. Vivid descriptions such as the examples we have shown contain the detailed information needed to extract a motivational pattern.

# CHAPTER EIGHT

# Five Ingredients

HAVING written and spoken about your enjoyable achievement experience, you are ready to discover your motivational pattern. Before examining your data, you need to know more about the five ingredients found in every motivational pattern, including yours. Each person's combination of these ingredients gives his or her approach to work and living a unique stamp. The ingredients and examples are listed below.

1. *Central motivational result*. This is a particular outcome or payoff of critical importance to you which you accomplish in essentially every one of your achievements. Here are some examples:

Something was built.

Difficulties were overcome.

Projects were completed.

Proficiency was attained.

2. *Motivated abilities*. You use certain abilities in reaching the central motivational result. For example:

Writing

Analyzing

Designing

Negotiating

Teaching

3. *Recurring subject matter*. You continue to receive satisfaction when working with your favorite subject matter. Subject matter might include:

Ideas

Money

A method

People

4. *Motivating circumstances*. You find yourself motivated in specific circumstances. For instance, you are motivated:

When competition is present.

When working to meet a need.

When involved with projects.

When a goal is present.

5. *Operating relationship*. People have a characteristic way of relating to others. For example, they may operate

in the position of leader;

best independently ;

as part of a team effort;

by manipulating others.

Let us now look at each ingredient in greater depth to help you understand how each functions in a motivational pattern.

## CENTRAL MOTIVATIONAL RESULT

The outcome of each achievement activity is of great importance; and when you examine your series of achievements, you'll find the payoff is always similar. Whether your achievements are spread over 10 or 50 years, are obviously related or apparently disparate, you consistently achieve the same central motivational result.

Each of us has a central motivational result we seek through our achievements. Once you discover your objective, you will find it evident in every achievement activity you recall. Below is a list of some possible central motivational results.

*Acquire / Possess — Money / Things / Status / People.* Wants to have own baby, to own toys, bicycles, houses, furniture, family, and so on . . . .

*Be in Charge / Command — Others / Things / Organization.* Wants to be on top, in authority, in the saddle—where it can be determined how things will be done . . . .

*Combat / Prevail — Over Adversaries / Evil / Opposing Philosophies.* Wants to come out against the bad guys, entrenched status quo, old technology . . . .

*Develop / Build — Structures / Technical Things.* Wants to make something where there was nothing . . . .

*Excel / Be the Best Versus Others / Conventional Standards.* Wants to be the fastest, first, longest, earliest, or more complicated, better than others . . . .

*Exploit / Achieve Potential — Situations / Markets / Things / People.* Sees a silk purse, a giant talent, a hot product, or a promising market before the fact . . . .

*Gain Response / Influence Behavior — From People / Throught People.* You want dogs, cats, people, and groups to react to your touch . . . .

*Gain Recognition / Attention — From Peers / Public Authority.* You want to wave at the cheering crowd, appear in the newspaper, be known, dance in the spotlight . . . .

*Improve / Make Better — Self / Others / Work / Organizations.* Make what is marginal, good; what is good, better; what makes a little money, make a lot of money . . . .

*Make the Team / Grade — Established by Others or System.* Gains access to the varsity, Eagle Scout rank, Silver Circle, Thirty-ninth Masonic Order, the country club, executive dining room . . . .

*Meets Needs / Fulfills Expectations — Demanded / Needed / Inherent.* Strives to meet specifications, shipping schedules, what the customer wants, what the boss has expressed . . . .

*Make Work / Make Effective — Things / Systems / Operations.* Fixes what is broken, changes what is out-of-date, redesigns what has been poorly conceived . . . .

*Master / Perfect—Subject / Skill / Equipment / Objects.* Goes after rough edges, complete domination of a technique, total control over the variables . . . .

*Organize / Operate — Business / Team / Product Line.* The entrepreneur, the beginner of new businesses . . . .

*Overcome / Persevere — Obstacles / Handicaps / Unknown Odds.* Goes after hungry tigers with a popgun, concave mountains with slippery boots . . . .

*Pioneer / Explore — Technology / Cultures / Ideas.* Presses through established lines, knowledge, boundaries . . . .

*Serve / Help — People / Organizations / Causes.* Carries the soup, ministers to the wounded, helps those in need . . . .

*Shape / Influemce — Material / Policy / People.* Wants to leave a mark, to cause change, to impact . . . .

A friend of ours, Richard N. Bolles, prepared the following analysis of his ideal job as he read through the various chapters and followed the instructions to the exercises. Dick Bolles is a master at reducing ideas to practical application and achieves a high level of detail and clarity we can all emulate.

## Defining My Ideal Job

I am:

*Contributor*—Like to do things that do not depend on others.

*Influencer*—Like to get others started, impact them, helping them to do a better job.

Like research, systematizing, improving, seeking usable knowledge, educating. I like problems, challenges, teaching the average person how to beat the system, with emphasis on the effectiveness of what I produce. Like to create wonder in people, produce a service, prefer a ministry with people through writing. Presentation, style, and media are key mechanisms. I like to influence, train, counsel, motivate, and delight people. I like applause and changed lives as a result of my work. I like mixing and synthesizing disciplines. I like to build up personal mastery of a subject, then find new and /or better ways to apply this knowledge to solve problems, master challenges. I like my end product to be an addition to knowledge and affect others, through its application and use with practical problems in their lives (and mine).

If I have a boss, I like him/her to be hands off but readily available, supportive, let me define desireable results out of trust for my abilities, values and common sense.

If I have subordinates, I prefer equals who are competent, neither stubborn nor over-yielding.

I prefer to work in circumstances where there is some certainty, some ambiguity, a relaxed atmosphere which is results-oriented, and I can be a reasonable risk-taker who makes devoted (but not do-or-die) efforts, where I can stand alone, invent new stuff, and manage my own career as a change-agent.

To fulfill my motivational pattern, I need a job working with people, words, pictures, and ideas. I require opportunities to analyze, organize, synthesize, and teach, which have the end result of recognition of my contribution and changed lives.

Two case studies will demonstrate the consistency with which a dominant central motivational result occurs during a lifetime. They may help you become aware of the kind of evidence to look for when trying to discover your own central motivational result. Both of these individuals' results clustered around having an effect. In the first case, the effect is on things and in the second case, on people.

## Mr. Fix-It

The recurring concern of this man is to make things work properly. He approaches every object with the question: "How can I make this thing work or work better?" If you examine the following achievement activities you will find evidence of this central motivational result.

Prepared pin mechanism on ream binder so that bundles would be tied. I was greatly satisfied to learn the tying mechanism, find the cause of the nontying and solve the problem in a simple fashion. Was completely satisfied—the fact that I found the solution to it and made it work . . . Completely disassembled a stopwatch and reassembled it after replacing the broken springs. The accomplishment was being able to put it back together and make it work . . . I derived satisfaction in being able to prove the structure quickly, in a simple way, by an approach that I thought of. What I liked about it was that I thought it up myself and that it worked . . . Discovered a reaction which gave useful chemicals. It was useful to other chemists in the group—they applied it in their work. Satisfaction—did give something useful . . .

## *Look, Ma, No Hands!*

Now, let us look at the achievement activities of someone who wants to have an impact on others; he wants to impress them and get a response.

Learning to read and write before going to grade school—it opened a lot of doors for me. Class clown—get up in front of a group of people and make them laugh . . . Played in the class play. Wasn't the lead role, but I got a fantastic ovation . . . Spoke at a few dinners—was the M.C.—telling the jokes between the acts. Really fun to keep it alive . . . Student taught for very tough critic teacher. I opened the door to hear him say, "He's got them eating right out of his hand." School wound up offering me a job. I got it from the kids, too, saying, "We thank you; glad you were my English teacher." . . . Had a summer job with a large steel company as a foreman. Was offered a job at the end of the summer because they liked my performance. Something about getting a job offer that makes me feel awfully good.

Many theories speculate that motivations are transitory and elusive. Yet we have found that *each person has a central drive dominating his or her behavior.* A central motivational result or payoff directs this voluntary behavior.

## MOTIVATED ABILITIES

The abilities a person uses when motivated are another ingredient of the motivational pattern. Most people's patterns contain five to eight abilities, but some have more. Each person also has abilities that lie outside his or her pattern; we call these skills "can do" abilities. If circumstance forces a person to use these abilities, he or she can perform acceptably, but at a level below that which occurs when using abilities that are part of his or her pattern. People are not motivated to use abilities outside their motivational pattern and will excel only when using motivated abilities.

Identifying motivated abilities is done by adding up recurring words used in an individual's descriptions of achievements required to excel at a task tend to group naturally within a person's pattern. The following is a list of abilities presented as they unfold in a typical achievement.

- Learning and Fact-Finding Abilities (reading, inquiring, researching)
- Evaluating Abilities (assessing worth, comparing to standard, decision making)
- Visualizing Abilities (setting goals, forming strategies, scheduling)
- Planning Abilities (setting goals, forming strategies, scheduling)
- Organizing Abilities (structuring, gathering details, categorizing)
- Developing/Creating Abilities (doing, crafting, assembling)

- Producing Abilities (acting, presenting, speaking)
- Overseeing Abilities (coordinating, facilitating, monitoring)
- Influencing Abilities (persuading, communicating, teaching)

Each of us seeks opportunities to use our motivated abilities and we will try to use these abilities even when the situation does not call for them. A person motivated to teach will strive to do so whether or not the skill is needed. A person motivated to innovate will innovate even when it is not appropriate. Someone motivated to "put the house in order" will do so, though others consider it a low priority. *Our perception of needs to be done is influenced by what we are motivated to accomplish.* We will try to reshape our jobs so we can do what we want, not necessarily what we are paid to do.

To illustrate how you can conclude that an ability is present, let us examine the achievement activities of three clients that reflect the existence of motivated abilities from the previous list. Italics provide clues to the motivational pattern.

### The Ability to Develop

Bought feeders, poultry, and *raised* them completely—a thousand chickens, a hundred turkeys, hundred ducks per year. . . . *Built* all of the houses and pens; *set up* a brooder area for the young birds. . . . *Building* my own rig, blinds, decoys. . . . *Developing* areas—*building* from the point of view of everyone in the office. . . . One thing I like to do is garden—started *raising* lettuce—*planting* a seed and seeing it *grow*.

### The Ability to Influence

At ages five and six—being able to *read aloud.* . . . *Ran convention* in fifth grade. Put on *demonstration* for student body—convinced myself I didn't have any problem *speaking* before large audience. . . . *Convincing* fellows they really could play ball. *Convince* them they ought to get together and practice. *Put pressure* on fellows who had athletic ability. . . . Sales job to try to *sell* the fraternity. Had to come to Washington and *explain* to people running this why it was necessary—had to *convince* them. . . . I had to *convince* some of the engineers to collect data. I *convinced* them they ought to pull that model out. Get all these guys in a room—*talk to them.*

### The Ability to Organize

*Organized* neighborhood kids. Put on a fair—*rounding up* kittens and rabbits—called the *Organizer.* . . . *Setting up* filing systems. . . . Got a group of *people together.* *Organized* an investment club. Bringing in speakers. *Bring it together.* Getting a group of *people together.* *Set up* a schedule. . . . One of four women who *organized* Columbus chapter of the national organization. *Organizing* the foods, church, clothing—get everything ready right down to the last.

... Had to *redesign the layout. How* you file up to the food area—roped it off—people coming down center aisles and fanning out.

After reading these examples, you should have an idea of what to look for when reviewing your achievement activities for motivated abilities in your motivational pattern.

## RECURRING SUBJECT MATTER

Another ingredient included in a motivational pattern is the subject matter with which an individual is motivated to work; this usually involves three to five items. After examining hundreds of patterns, We have found that subject matter often falls into the categories listed below.

- Intangibles (ideas, principles, values)
- Tangibles (materials, tools, structures)
- Data (numbers, words, symbols)
- People (individuals, groups, behavior)
- Technical (science, engineering, math)
- Sensory (shapes, sounds, colors)
- Methods (systems, strategies, models)

For example the person motivated to work with *people* and not tangible things or date may perform housework marginally and handle banking ineffectively, but would be a treasured resource in the neighborhood for dealing with relational problems. The secretary motivated to work with *details* but not *people* would have strong clerical skills but would have less interest in the relational aspects of the job.

Examine the subject matter indicated by italics in the two individuals' achievement activities that follow. Later you will see what your own achievements reveal.

### *Tangible Subject Matter*

Dismantle *clock*. ... Making *scooters* out of orange crates. ... Wind-up *phonograph*. ... *Air conditioner* on my car. ... Hudson automobile *engine*— tear the the *engine* down—make measurements on all the parts. ... All principal systems of *submarine*: power, propulsion, ballasting, trim, ventilation, heating. Loosened *bolts coupling* misaligned—went to *machine shop* for stock. Aligned *shafts* experimentally. ... Troubleshooting on Navy *electronic equipment*. Built self-contained, completely controllable pulse *generator* to drive up to one hundred radars. ... Build dual-time code *decoder* and buffer.

## Methods Subject Matter

*Reorganized* the college bookstore in *supermarket style*. *System* I developed is still being used today. . . . Salvaged a production-control *system*. . . . Coordinated the *longest land move* of Marine Division in Korea. Developed a practical *system* for controlling manufacturing operations. *Organized* the PERT office. . . Developed the Cost Index *System*. Participated in symposium on management *systems*. . . . Developed a *system* for following ADP work orders.

We have found that understanding your subject matter is a good place to start when making career decisions. You need to know what subject matter turns you into a motivated worker.

## MOTIVATING CIRCUMSTANCES

The motivational pattern also contains situationally specific circumstances under which an individual is motivated. Although you can categorize this part of the pattern in a variety of ways, I have found the following to be helpful.

- Competitive Circumstances (competition, testing, combative)
- Triggering Circumstances (needs, problems, causes)
- Structured Circumstances (ordered, fluid, or scripted situations)
- Visible Circumstances (audiences, notoriety, recognition)
- Measured Circumstances (finished produce, goals, potential for profit)
- Environmental or Organizational Circumstances (autocratic, participative, political, results oriented)

The conditions that initiate motivated behavior vary greatly from person to person. Some are triggered into action when confronted by a need while others are attracted to head-to-head competition or emergency situations. For example, the salesperson, accountant, or industrial engineer motivated to work on *problems* will invent one to solve if one does not already exist. The person motivated to work on *projects* will structure any task regardless if it can be handled efficiently that way. The person animated by *stress*, competition, combat, adversity or trouble, gravitates to aspects of his or her work that involve high intensity. If motivated conditions are not present, little effort is exerted except that caused by such an inherent threat as losing a source of income.

As with other motivational pattern ingredients, the presence of a motivating circumstance in achievement activities is determined by adding up words of similar meaning. Examine the following examples taken from two clients' achievement activities; note the italics.

## Competitive Circumstances

Liked to *test* myself—liked to take *tests*. . .. Never avoided the opportunity of *testing* myself. I like to get called in to help *solve a problem*. Then in became a *detective game* to find out what had really happened. . . . Welcomed the opportunity in junior high school for athletic *competition*. . . . One of the *competitions* that I invariably entered and enjoyed was spelling. . . . I enjoyed the *completion*. Could relate a dozen instances in which I have been the focal point of some *critical activity* in which a lot hangs in the balance. . . . *Competitive* flying.

## Triggering Circumstances

We *needed* the food. Greatest satisfaction was bringing home *food for the family*. . . . Especially rewarding to be able to *do something for country*. . . *Battled the flood* of 1955—helped resume production two days later. . . . *Enjoyed getting people out to vote*. . . . Worked to help *support* my family—managed my father's store while he was hospitalized . . .. Satisfaction was having a nice home to *meet the needs* of family. . . . Gave me a great deal of satisfaction to develop a fabric which would give continuity of production, and this was a *sorely needed* staple.

Your achievement activities will reveal the specific circumstances that captivate you. Understanding this dynamic ingredient of your motivational pattern will be a key to a productive and fulfilling life.

# OPERATING RELATIONSHIPS

The final ingredient of the motivational pattern is how you naturally operate with others. When you examine your achievement activities, you will find you seek a particular role or relationship with others. For example, one person consistently does things alone, another works as part of a group or team, another person seeks the role of manager, and someone else wants to act as a coach or advisor for others.

Many questions asked by organizations and families can be answered by knowing the individual's operating relationship.

- Who runs this place, you or me?
- Why do we fight so much when we work together?
- Can she organize her part of town?
- Can she be a secretary to several executives?
- Can he handle others without line authority?
- People like her, but can she manage?

Answers to questions of this type are available by discovering the desired operating relationships in the achievement activities of those involved. Interactions between people are determined by this aspect of their motivational pattern.

Over the course of examining hundreds of clients, I found three broad categories to describe the way people build relationships. These categories are flexible enough to accommodate the unique operating relationship that motivates each individual.

1. *Contributor*—People whose work does not depend on making others take action; such as an individualist, a team member, or a star.

2. *Influencer*—People who cause others to take action but don't want overall responsibility for confronting others and dealing with adversity; such as an enabler, a coach, or a coordinator.

3. *Manager*—People who put others' talents to use to accomplish a goal or get something done, or a manager.

A person may fit into just one of the categories or may be a combination of two. For example, when operating alone the person is a *contributor*; but becomes a *manager* when working with a group because he or she uses people as an extension of his or her individualism.

In addition to these categories, each person is comfortable in a certain operating relationship with the authority figures in his or her life. Some people want close, supportive relationships, others want their leaders to point them in a direction and then get out of the way, and still others will work only for people who treat them as equals.

The following cases from our files reveal different types of operating relationships. Here, as elsewhere in the process of identifying the motivational pattern, you should have added up key words from the individual's achievement activities. My conclusions are indicated by the case headings. Note the italics in the edited quotes.

## Togetherness—A Team Member

*We* did something every waking hour. . . . *We* used to skate and maneuver in all those people. . . . Exploring new areas *with two or three friends*. Built them *ourselves*—done in *group*. . . . *My friends and I* used to fix things up. *We* all had bicycles. . . . *We* built rafts—*my brother and I*. All pulled *together*. Always kind of a *cooperative* thing—there was no leader—usually a *mutual* kind of thing. . . Bride and I *worked together* where it took two. Designed *our* own house—of course my wife *worked with me*. . . . One of *my friends and I* started small business. Talking with my boss, *we* got idea. . . . Head editorial *committee*. Got friendly with lexicographer—*we worked together*. . . . *Committee* to make determination of proper definitions—oftentimes *we* said, "No, that's not what that word means." . . . Enjoyed *working with* the men who had gained prominence in my chosen field. . . . I was *one of the team*—the *camaraderie* among us. We spent all afternoon discussing what *we* should do.

### *Doing It Myself—An Individualist*

*I* learned to speak English—learned it *secretly*. . . .*I* gave the best talk of the year in fourth grade.. . *I* invented solution to problem on test. Did a lot of studying *alone* in areas other than school assigned. . . . Found *I* could win easily on either side of debating issue. *I beat the system*. Steel mill having problem—everyone was standing around in a puzzled way. Popped into *my mind* that there was not sufficient water to permit acid to fully ionize. Said, Why don't you add several hundred gallons? . . . Asked to write lead paper—it allowed *me* to emphasize the *unconventional* areas *I* had. *I* was able to put it all together into this "healing" concept. . . .*I* evolved curriculum, found teachers—administration gave *me* a building. *I* was jokingly referred to as the Dean. . . . *With no help*, *I* planned and erected a two-room addition to *my house*. . . . Transferred—move into new home and did all *my own fixing up*. Special gratification in having done it *myself*.

Notice how naturally each person's speech reveals a consistent way they relate to others. You probably did not strain for the conclusions in either case. Your consistent operating relationship will also become apparent when you look at your achievement activities.

## PATTERNS ARE A SYSTEM OF MOTIVATED BEHAVIOR

At this point, I want to emphasize a crucial feature of motivational patterns: a pattern operates as an intricate system and its ingredients cannot function independently of one another. though I divided a pattern into its five ingredients for discussion and described each one separately, please remember that each must be perceived in the context of the others; each ingredient enables, defines, and modifies the other four. In other words, a person uses his or her motivated abilities to work with his or her subject matter within specific motivating circumstances and operating relationships to achieve a central motivational result. Motivated behavior cannot be understood unless the interdependency of the ingredients is considered.

Now that you are acquainted with the five ingredients of your motivational pattern and their systemic nature, let's look at the nature of your pattern and how it captures your very essence.

# CHAPTER NINE
# Your Design Is Your Essence

WHEN WE discuss the concept of your design, or what we have called your motivational pattern, it is easy to envision it as a component of you (as if it could exist separately from you!) Actually, you *are* your motivational pattern, it is not just an internal program. You think, express, and act with such consistency that when your approach to these activities is described, the description is your identity. You should never talk about your pattern as if ingredients could be changed, like getting new tires for the car. Nor should it be referred to as a "program" over which you have no control. Your pattern does not make you do anything. It reveals the complex way you accomplish what you do when you act voluntarily; your pattern is the manifestation of your will.

You can always decide not to act and that is your will. You can also decide to do (or refrain from doing) what you are being asked or compelled by others to do. However, if you are free or able to function in accordance with your will, and you decide to act, you will act in accordance with your pattern.

This kind of language seems to support the philosophy of determinism. However, many people are uncomfortable with the conclusion that human actions are inevitable because each of us is driven by a pattern. Humans are capable of making *genuine* decisions. You should not believe all your decisions are inevitable. You decide certain things should happen and they wouldn't happen unless you made that decision. The pattern describes how you exercise your decision-making power and the situations that become the stage for enacting those decisions. So, while we recognize the human ability to make decisions, we also recognize pattern's influence on our decision-making processes.

Some individuals, especially those with motivated abilities in developing people, such as teachers, coaches, and counselors, claim they can accomplish anything they *decide* to do. We agree because they will only genuinely decide to do those things that emerge from who they are fundamentally. Now, if they claim they can do anything, we would protest. But even the person who believes that no restrictions limit what they can become will not claim that they can do anything at all. Why? They know they will never have the interest to do certain activities.

Stating that you are your pattern is helpful to clarify that your pattern is not something you possess. But do not conclude that your motivational pattern describes your entire personality. We know that patterns are an important factor of being an individual; but the human personality is extremely complex and we do not claim that patterns can answer all the questions you have about yourself. Patterns have little to say about character and moral issues—such as honesty, loyalty or justice. But understanding the power of your motivational pattern will provide you with considerable self-knowledge. We are excited to share our discoveries about the characteristics of patterns in the pates that follow.

## THE EARLY EMERGENCE AND CONSISTENCY OF MOTIVATIONAL PATTERNS

A person comes into the world with his or her motivational pattern intact. Our opinion about this is based on many observations that refute the influence on behavior credited to environmental factors. We have found no correlation between motivational patterns and the environment in which an individual was raised. For example, siblings raised by parents in the same environment turn out wonderfully unique. People who participate in similar activities while growing up have diverse behavior patterns as adults.

In addition, the complex and system pattern is manifested during preschool before any formal educational training. Young children exhibit a precociousness when they use their motivated abilities; yet they struggle when required to perform tasks that do not engage their gifts. Finally, we believe patterns are innate because we have never encountered a client who acquired a motivational gift not possessed since childhood.

Most people recall an achievement activity from as early as five or six years old, some can remember back to age three or four, and a few people describe experiences that occurred even earlier. At whatever age achievement activities start, a behavior pattern is well fleshed out by at least one's late teens. Your motivational pattern matures through the demands of increasingly complex achievement activities as you grow, but its essence remains consistent. During your lifetime, you will find that nothing significant is added or removed from your pattern's core, in spite of changes in life style and values. Advanced education, prosperity, being a prisoner of war, a personal tragedy, or a peak experience cannot change the fundamental ingredients of your motivational pattern, though other aspects of your personality may be profoundly affected. This consistency is a tremendous asset because it enables you to plan your development without the fear that you will become fundamentally different in five years from who you are now.

## PATTERNS ARE IRREPRESSIBLE

You continually attempt to exercise your motivational pattern in spite of environmental sterility or repression. The reality you perceive is shaped by the pattern; it affects how you approach your work. When the motivational value of a task or role has been exhausted, you will seek a new focus or arena in which to express your strengths. You may slump into despondency if circumstances collude to prevent your pattern's expression over a long period of time. The pattern explains how you will attempt to order any situation to receive personal satisfaction. You will resist conflicting demands and may destroy conventional expectations when they do not align with your intentions.

## BEHAVIOR IS INFLUENCED BY MOTIVATIONAL PATTERNS

When involved in an activity that does not motivate you, your behavior is different from that displayed when you are doing something that is motivating. The difference occurs because motivated behavior reflects your will and giftedness while unmotivated behavior does not. Unmotivated behavior is powered by external forces such as social values and personal relationships. Statements such as "I ought to do this though I don't want to," or, "My supervisor would be disappointed if I don't do this," are indicative of behavior grounded outside the motivational pattern.

In our opinion, most theories of behavior are unsound because they fail to accept the duality involved in an individual's behavior. For example, the concept of introversion/extroversion is not as useful as it could be because it does not distinguish between motivated and unmotivated activities. Seemingly contradictory behavior can be easily explained by understanding motivational patterns. The person motivated to sell, perform, teach, or coach can be outgoing when participating in those activities but may be withdrawn and antisocial when not involved in such activities.

Much of the investigation into human motivations has sought a standard principle to explain whether people are pulled or pushed into action and once motivated, what sustains that behavior. Answers to this question are idiosyncratic to each person and can be revealed by understanding that person's motivational pattern.

One person is triggered into motivated behavior when confronted by a problem or head-to-head competition. Another person's motivated behavior is initiated by an idea that seems sensible and causes him or her to speculate about new directions. A third person plunges into motivated behavior when asked for help, the ground rules are clear, and the standards for performance and timetable have been established. The causes of motivated behavior can be a single factor or a set of them; can be initiated by circumstances, by other people, or within the achiever; can result in a predetermined goal or involve an uncertain process that may go noplace. The answers are always unique to each person resulting from his or her motivational pattern; and no standard principle is useful for predicting what will motivate all individuals.

Similarly, the choice of how much energy to exert depends on factors in each person's motivational pattern. People whose central motivational result is to meet a personal challenge can be expected to put out any amount of energy required by the goal. Those whose central motivational result focuses on competing with or impressing others can be expected to expend only the effort necessary to surpass the opponent or to make an impact. If people are primarily concerned with obtaining tangible results, the amount of effort required to gain those results can be assured.

Even if most of the motivating ingredients are present, some people are willing to put forth significant effort only if they know that when the task or project is completed they will receive a valued reward. Variations of this are endless. Common elements a person can use to weigh the value the reward has for them personally against the required effort are the time frame of the payback, the specificity of reward, the personal or professional risk, the presence or absence of structure, the caliber of competition, whether or not the challenge or reward is new to them, and the nature of the organization.

However, even after taking into account a wide range of possible incentives, the notion that a reward is an absolute prerequisite for motivated behavior is not true. Many people are process oriented: they are content to participate in activities without distinct expectations for the outcome. People often become engaged in activities that have no foreseeable conclusion, much less cheering crowds or monetary gain. The motivation to pioneer is an example of an activity that does not provide expectations for specific conclusions or results. A motivation to develop a concept and to explore new areas of knowledge are examples of process-oriented drives that might have terminus but supply little recognition, reward, or response. The satisfaction provided by many achievement activities is the process itself.

## MOTIVATIONAL PATTERNS AND SOCIAL BEHAVIOR

The motivational pattern is reflected in all areas of an individual's life. Not only is it revealed in a way a person approaches tasks, it can be seen at work in aspects of one's social life that, at first, appear to be merely a matter of personal taste or style. For example, in conversation, the person motivated to impress others may relive a trip to a war-torn country. A person motivated to meet needs may encourage another to reveal a current difficulty and then offer counsel. Someone motivated to prevail intuitively moves toward a weakness revealed in another's position. A person motivated to interact one-on-one makes an intense conversationalist. Advocates are known for sermonizing while performers are known for their liveliness and wit.

Even the manner of dress reveals a person's giftedness and motivation. Strict conformity to an unwritten dress code shows the desire to be accepted; smartness, reflecting a great deal of care, reveals the motivation to impress; the bizarre dresser wants to be different; the man who wears white socks with a dark suit indicates his lack of concern with appearance; and the woman a half-step ahead of what is fashionable reveals her ability to anticipate trends.

The formation and outcome of personal relationships is also highly dependent on an individual's motivational pattern. Some people are motivated to cultivate close, egalitarian relationships; their friends feel they play a important role in life. People who attempt to shape others have a history of transient relationships with younger, inexperienced individuals. Those persons motivated to overcome obstacles may look back and find a series of relationships with losers. Similarly, motivational elements reflecting a desire for filling needs, eliteness, controlling situations, exploiting potential, uniqueness, team membership, and a chance to demonstrate personal expertise all find their expression in the kind and length of relationships a person forms.

Conflict in boss-employee, co-workers, teacher-student, husband-wife, parent-child, counselor-client, and/or union-company relationships frequently can be traced to the motivational patterns of the combatants. Understanding the other's motivational pattern often leads the way to resolution. Examples can be found in every kind of relationship: an individualist wife married to a team-member husband; a counselor who wants to teach advising a client who wants to learn on his own; a hands-on boss supervising employees motivated to operate independently; an employee who desires a supportive boss working for an employer who is not motivated to work with people; a union representative motivated to win negotiating with a management representative motivated to prevail; an employee motivated to bring things to completion teamed with a detail-oriented co-worker; or the employee who attempts to meet all the requirements working with someone motivated to be a pioneer.

## YOUR MIND FUNCTIONS IN ACCORDANCE
## WITH YOUR MOTIVATIONAL PATTERN

Your motivational pattern affects *how* you learn; *what* subjects you learn; *why* you learn; *whether* you learn in a team setting, alone, or in a team setting after independently acquiring background knowledge. Similarly, it determines the significance you place on what was learned, the depth of knowledge acquired, and the role the knowledge plays in your behavior.

Not only is your learning determined by your motivational pattern so is your ability to evaluate and make decisions, and to plan, organize, create, conceive, and design.

The influence of your motivational pattern helps determine how you perceive a job should be done. You will probably not try to perform a job according to the job description or supervisor's expectations unless these external factors match your motivational pattern: a person motivated to innovate will try to innovate; someone motivated to control will set up controls; an individual motivated to overcome problems will find problems; someone to build relationships will attempts this; and someone motivated to expand the boundaries will start breaking the edges. People motivated to produce visible evidence of their effort will move toward projects with the potential for visible completion. People motivated to prove others wrong will go after competing work that is suspect, shallow or incomplete. A supervisor motivated to shape others enjoys training inexperienced subordinates but will continue to try to mold them after they have considerable experience. A salesperson motivated to build from scratch will select an apparently barren territory over a financially established territory. People motivated to bring chaos to order will gravitate to those parts of their jobs where confusion reigns.

## THE FUNCTION OF ENVIRONMENT IN
## MOTIVATED BEHAVIOR

In over 25 years of counseling, we have never interviewed a person with a motivated ability that's been created by an environmental influence. Outside influences range from teachers and significant life experiences, to peer and parental pressure. These external forces cannot change your gift. Nothing can happen to you that will create new motivated abilities.

However, environmental influences play a critical role in developing motivational patterns. For example, some people's patterns motivate them to learn and to be taught by someone. Even when the desire to learn is part of the pattern, many external variables resulting from the interaction of the student's and teacher's patterns enter into the process of motivated learning and set up a series of conditions that must be met before learning can take place. Examples of types of conditions required for an individual to learn from a specific teacher include such things as gaining a favorable response from the teacher, meeting the expectations of the teacher, or prevailing against a teacher's negative predictions; figuring out the teacher's style and developing a learning strategy; being stimulated by the teacher; having the teacher express a sincere interest; working with the teacher as a team member; listening to the teacher lecture; or discussing material with the teacher as an equal. The possible conditions necessary for motivated learning to take place are limitless because of the unique combination of patterns created by each student and teacher.

Generalizing about motivated learning would be an error; each person interacts differently with environmental circumstances to develop his or her motivational pattern. We have already discussed the unique relationship required by each student and teacher to promote learning. A person may insist on learning "by myself." Our studies show that people most frequently are comfortable learning by doing. Others use a method of reading and reflection or a process of exploration and observation. Whatever role environment plays in motivated learning, it must meet the needs established by an individual's motivational pattern. One person may need a teacher and another enjoys the stimulation of directing his or her own learning.

What is true of learning is true of other motivated behavior such as creating, developing, problem solving, and decision making. Environment can be critical. Sometimes environment precipitates behavior; for example, a person may be motivated to act only when confronted by a problem or a need. Sometimes environment is the source of inspiration, as it is for landscape painters. Other times it is used as a data base (perhaps for a theoretical mathematician or physicist).

People in authority have been credited with causing motivated behavior. However, even situational circumstances that are necessary elements in a person's motivated behavior do not cause the behavior. Again generalizations about types of circumstances that motivate behavior do not apply —some persons require triggering circumstances, some require triggering circumstances, some require structured circumstances, some require circumstances that produce visibility, some require circumstances that produced measurable results. The role of environmental influence on the motivated behavior of people cannot be captured by governing principles, but only through examining the individual case. Admittedly, environmental forces have a powerful impact on behavior. They can influence the direction and quality of a life, a person's interests and values, and the level of achievement. But regardless of the strength of external factors, the motivational pattern still forms the basis for a person's behavior. We have found that the conqueror will always seek opportunities to overcome whether he or she is a brain surgeon, a shortstop, or a construction engineer, and the person motivated to be an entrepreneur will always be motivated in this direction whether he or she is a priest, a civil servant, a dentist, or the owner of a business.

## MOTIVATIONAL PATTERNS AND VALUE SYSTEMS

A person can use his or her motivational pattern either constructively or destructively. Knowledge of patterns has not been helpful for predicting actions that involve issues of integrity, loyalty, or honesty. A thief can be gifted; genius can purvey drugs. Our personal value systems do not appear to be related to our gifts and motivations. How we use what we have been given is a separate issue. The person carrying a placard to support a cause he or she finds motivationally significant is not necessarily more virtuous than the entrepreneur working to make a profit or the farmer attempting to increase a crop yield; each is following his or her motivational pattern to gain personal satisfaction.

Having said this, we must also add that many people take a particular social or moral stance because it is required if they are to continue participating in activities that engage their motivational patterns. If they did not make their opinions known, their achievement activities might be regulated or repressed by law or social standards in the future. They may support a regulated economy, police dogs, or a strict city-zoning policy to ensure that they can maintain the life-style they are motivated to pursue. They may become involved in a local or regional environmental cause because the outcome will affect whether or not they can continue to participate in recreational activities they find personally fulfilling. They may sacrifice evenings and weekends to solicit votes for a political candidate who promises to tighten the budget or whose stance on abortion is pro-choice. People will take a moral stance to protect their right to exercise their motivational patterns even if they are not consciously aware of it or its nature.

## USING MOTIVATIONAL PATTERNS
## TO PREDICT BEHAVIOR

A person's behavior in any job or role can be predicted by identifying the motivational pattern as it unfolds during an achievement activity. The person will perceive and attempt to function in any work, domestic, or social situation in accordance with his or her pattern. Depending on the individual's motivational ingredients, for example, he or she will learn by asking a lot of questions, jumping into the tasks involved, trying to obtain an overall picture about expectations, strategically planning the details for getting the job done, or spending a lot of time reviewing the numbers and formulating answers for questions likely to be asked. The person will conform automatically to his or her behavior pattern and distort the job to the extent this is permitted; the pattern is reflected not only by what is tackled buy by what is avoided or given only superficial attention.

If a complete description of the critical job requirements and the motivational dynamics of the boss and other employees can be obtained, we can predict how an individual will interact with the others and how he or she will face special circumstances and demands. Unfortunately, few businesses can provide such description. Regardless of situational dynamics, a person will consistently attempt to follow his or her motivational pattern. When pressed to alter the behavior, the person will cling to the tendencies rooted in his or her pattern, even when it is disruptive and unacceptable. For example, a new regional sales manager who makes decisions through lengthy collaboration may look foolish in staff meetings if he or she asks others for opinions when the facts have just been presented. Or a plant manager who works on an annual cycle carefully gathering data before making product and market decisions, will appear inflexible to the new boss who wants to continually fine tune and change direction midstream. If a person who has to thoroughly evaluate a matter before coming to a decision is given an assignment requiring a quick response, he or she may try to find a way to push back the deadline by requesting more data or arranging meetings with the staff. Such maneuvers will be viewed negatively, though the behavior could have been predicted if the motivational behavior had been considered. Expressed in terms of motivated behavior, these persons continue to try to assimilate new situations into their behavioral patterns, even risking their jobs, rather than adopting a new style. They are more concerned with doing what is comfortable than with how their actions appear to others.

In the remaining chapters we will help you learn how to predict your behavior and the behavior of those around you, and to use this knowledge to find the jobs and relationships that best match your motivational pattern.

ತಿ *Part Three* ತಿ

# Building Your Life
# on Your Gifts

CHAPTER TEN

# Career Implications of Your Design

THE WAY to make sound career decisions is to understand and apply your motivational pattern. It reveals the *working parameters* suitable for you and your career potential. If you realize that vocations which do not engage your strengths are wrong for you, you can screen out inappropriate job opportunities and focus on the promising ones.

Let's face it, our society is obsessed with getting ahead and going higher. Unfortunately, you can acquire a high position only to find that you have no desire to or cannot fill it once you have arrived. The focus should not be on whether you can reach a certain level but if you are effective and fulfilled in your career. As you work through the following material, we urge you to search for the truth about yourself and to identify career goals that match your strengths. In this chapter you will put to use the data you've gathered for each of the five ingredients to help you clarify your career direction. The order in which you'll move through the five sections corresponds to each ingredient's usefulness in helping to focus your search; subject matter, motivating circumstances motivated abilities, central motivational result, and motivated operating relationships. You will also determine whether your achievement activities suggest a role as a manager, an influencer, or a contributor.

## CAREER IMPLICATIONS OF YOUR
## MOTIVATIONAL PATTERN

### *What Your Subject Matter Says About You*

What are you motivated to work with: numbers, words, concepts, structural objects, colors, shapes, people, money, plants, animals, machinery, tools? You will seek out the three to five subject matter items you identified in Chapter 8 in every job situation. Try to find and remain in a career that emphasizes the subject matter with which you are motivated to work. Don't stay in a field or business if the subject matter only casually interests you.

Always seek compatibility between the product or service an employer provides and what you are motivated to work with. If you work as a nurse or a counselor, people ought to be one of the items in your motivated subject matter list. If the employer designs and manufactures electronic instruments, an interest in concepts or structural objects may be essential to your job satisfaction.

Beyond directing you to the general field, your motivated subject matter should be specifically required by the function in which you are employed. If you are considering underwriting insurance, numbers, concepts, and principles should be your interests. If a career involving computers is a possibility, symbols and systems ought to fascinate you. Also, closely examine the details of your subject matter. You may have taken a job because you enjoy working with people. But if you don't evaluate your interests carefully you may discover, too late, that you are required to develop one-on-one relationships while your strength is in working with groups.

The long-term career implications of what subject matter interest you depend upon the subjects' nature and breadth. Assuming that you possess managerial abilities, you can aim for executive positions if your motivated subjects include people; a data item such as numbers or dollars, an intangible such as concepts, ideas, or principles; and additional items that cover technical aspects the specific business requires.

A professional position may be a better career direction if your motivated subject matter is narrower and integrated, for instance, math, details, and scientific principles; or numbers, structures, and materials; or behavior phenomena, ideas, and instruments.

When you are trying to determine the right job for you, you first need to look at the functions or activity with which you think you might identify. Matching your strengths to a particular activity may be difficult because of the specialization of duties within a business. Often your motivated subject matter will form a cluster that readily suggests an activity. A clustering of concepts, phenomena, physical science, and information justifies exploring a career in research and development. A combination of numbers, money, policies, and controls warrants considering finance or accounting. Principles, instruments, details, and techniques might lead you toward testing services.

Another approach for matching your motivated subject matter to a career is to pretend you're a computer; do a series of sorts through several activities normally found in a business. Begin with your most general subject matter item, one that is required in several functions of businesses or organizations. For example, an interest in technology is essential for engineering, product development, and operations research. Then pick a second item from your subject matter and integrate it with your first selection. If the subject is materials, the combination becomes technological materials. Already the activities that may interest you begin to narrow: materials engineering and process development. Next, add a third subject. If structures interest you, the materials engineering still looks promising but the possibility of process development is less likely unless the products of the business are structural in nature.

## What Your Motivating Circumstances Say About You

The career planning process is aided by considering your motivating circumstances. Here the factors being considered are what triggers and sustains motivated behavior; the kind of structure, measurability, and visibility you require; the form and size of organization you find comfortable; the kind of organization and climate you find stimulating.

After narrowing your career possibilities with your motivated subject matter, sharpen your focus by applying your motivating circumstances to the tentative conclusions you have reached. For example, if a person is motivated to work on problems in an unstructured setting with some visibility and want to produce tangible or measurable results, he or she can probably screen out many activities in materials process engineering. From the combined information of these subject matter and motivating circumstances, working with clients whose sales are decreasing because of a problem with materials appears to be the type of situation this person would enjoy tackling.

## What Your Motivated Abilities Say About You

Since the majority of motivated abilities can be applied to hundreds of jobs, examining the career implications of your abilities is not very helpful in guiding you toward a specific vocation. Consider the ability to develop a strategic plan; this skill is useful in most professional or management positions. However, a review of some types of abilities can be helpful in drawing broad conclusions about your career.

Because your motivational learning style—how and why you are motivated to learn—is a fundamental skill affecting all forms of activities, it has critical career implications. Your learning style can determine whether or not you will excel in certain work roles. If a person learns only through a comprehensive process that requires much time and effort, he or she should be cautious about working in a position where limited time is available for resolving problems. Because of this person's learning style, he or she would probably perform more effectively in a staff position.

Similarly, people who learn by doing should concentrate on a specialty with established procedures or a position in which learning requirements at any point are limited. Hand-on learners may become discouraged in the higher levels of management because the learning requirements become increasingly abstract and diverse.

How you evaluate soundness or correctness or value also has career overtones. If you evaluate by analysis but do not have an ability for making decisions on complex, risky issues, you should seriously question becoming involved in a career that normally takes you into general management ranks. Similarly, if your ability to evaluate is constrained by needing a standard to measure against, consider those levels and roles that have such standards, normally lower than higher in most organizations.

Another related issue is how you plan. If your ability is in scheduling but does not include establishing goals or developing enabling strategies, you may find a hands-on role more suitable than one in management.

## What Your Central Motivational Result Says About You

As with motivated abilities, the central motivational result does not provide much guidance in narrowing your career choices. Most jobs accommodate the spectrum of results. For example, a police officer, a teacher, a metallurgist, and a plant manager could have the desire to excel, overcome, meet requirements, or gain a response as a central motivational thrust. Certain mismatched exceptions do exist, however, cost accounting and obtaining recognition, basic research and meeting requirements, staff personnel work and being in charge, executive management and gaining mastery are all like oil and water. Because some careers can't produce certain results, testing whether or not a proposed job will allow you to fulfill your central motivational result is necessary.

Now let us move to the final ingredient of the motivational pattern—how people operate with others.

## What Your Operating Relationships Say About You

Since childhood, any group of which you were a part had to solve the issue of who was the leader. The question, "Am I a leader or not?" requires an answer from everyone. Due to cultural, domestic, and economic pressures, the career decision having the most long-term significance is whether you pursue a career leading or managing others' contributions or one that relies on your own contribution.

### THE LEADER/MANAGER

Whether or not you have the ability to lead others is not dependent on your age; you are either comfortable and effective at leading or managing others or you're not. If people have looked to you for decisions in any sports, academic, domestic, community, or career activities the chances are likely that you are a leader or a manager or both. From early achievement activity data, we have found that managers were the children concerned with who was doing things, whether it was playing third base, cleaning the kitchen, selling tickers, designing posters, or delivering papers.

We have prepared a list of characteristics indicative of a good leader/manager. We feel that to be a good leader/manager, you should be good at and enjoy:

- Being in a position of authority.
- Helping others, individually and collectively, become more effective.
- Being held responsible for others' performance.
- Accomplishing goals through others' abilities.
- Confronting subordinates when you need to.
- Explaining you expectations.
- Developing long-term working relationships.
- Helping solve others' problems.
- Taking the time to listen.
- Sorting out arguments.
- Making the decision ultimately adopted.

## THE INFLUENCES

Some people appear to be leaders/ managers because they like to influence others; but they do not want to have continuing or overall responsibility for another's work. When you review your achievement activities, notice if you have set people into action even if you weren't in charge. If so, you may be an influencer. The way to determine if you are an influencer or a manager is whether you want to *follow up* on the actions of those you have influenced to make sure they complete things. A good way to test yourself is to ask whether or not you get a nervous stomach when you confront someone about poor performance.

A good career situation for an influenced is to oversee a staff of professionals where pure management activities are minimal and where there is a need to personally affect the clients.

## THE CONTRIBUTOR

Examining the characteristics that follow may help you decide if a career centered on your personal contribution rather than a management position is appropriate. If one or more of the characteristics on the list typifies your motivated behavior, seriously consider a career working within your specialty and avoid management or leadership roles.

- You like to work with information or things but not people, or to work with people but not information or things.
- You want to comprehend a matter thoroughly before acting on the information you obtain.
- You are excited by the opportunity to look at all sides of a proposal but have some difficulty making decisions.

- You love to work on complex tasks but aren't too concerned with deadlines or how much it will cost.
- You enjoy participating but don't care who wins.
- You want your work to have well-defined requirements.
- You are consistently a "bear" about detail.
- You feel you have to do things yourself if you want them done right.
- You only enjoy working with things you can hear, see, touch, or smell.
- You must have things done your way.
- You like to work alone.
- You like to work with others but don't want overall responsibility for the outcome.

Now that you've examined whether you are an influencer, manager, or contributor, or a combination of two of the three, let's move on and look at some career decisions.

# CHAPTER ELEVEN

# Defining Your Ideal Job

THERE ARE many issues to consider in the career-planning process. To help you focus on these issues, we have designed a short survey for you to complete. The answers to these questions will help you later in this chapter when you define your ideal job. Please don't be confused if you find you fall in more than one group when answering a question. People aren't put together quite as neatly as these classifications indicate. Relax in the fact that you have more flexibility than some of the rest of us.

Your response to any of the questions should be relatively obvious from the knowledge you have gained up to this point about your motivational pattern. If you are unclear on any point, return to your achievements and reread the relevant material. Issues posed in the questions are not normally complex. Circle that response which most closely matches your motivated behavior.

## THE CAREER CROSSROADS SURVEY

1. Are you a contributor, influencer, or manager?

A. *Contributor*—effort does not depend on requiring others to take action, although may be involved with team effort.

B. *Influencer*—effort concerned with getting things started, developing other, impacting on others, but not interested in overall or continuing management of others.

C. *Management*—effort concerned with getting things done through others by one or more managerial mechanisms; e.g., control and regulation; collaboration and mediation; leadership and management; detail plan or system.

2. Do you prefer being on the firing line or having support?

A. *On the firing line*—getting things done within tight time constraints; important to short-term survival of the organization; enjoy urgency and a pressure to produce; prefer sales, production, production control, recruiting, accounting, or purchasing.

B. *Having support*—helping someone else to do a better job; important to profitability, but not necessary to survival; working in a longer time-frame; like to have support, service, and control; need to improve and/or systematize; prefer marketing, research, salary administration, systems, product development, operations research, or organization development.

3. What is your preferred duration and focus of activity?

A. *Functional*—duration is ongoing; gratification usually associated with improvements in tangible or measurable results, prefer production, recruiting, purchasing, accounting, testing, or distribution.

B. *Research*—requirements are general; nature of work includes seeking exploitable knowledge; relatively long time periods; prefer basic fundamental research, psychoanalytic process, test development, drugs development, ecological impact studies, or education.

4. Is your emphasis on technical things, production, business, marketing or people?

A. *Technical*—concerned with science, engineering, methodology, problems, issues, knowledge; emphasis on research, development, and consulting; exactness and effectiveness are critical values.

B. *Production*—concerned with producing a product or service; sensitive to cost, value, quality, and efficiency considerations; short-term results; meeting standards, teamwork, pressure, and immediacy of problem solving are critical issues.

C. *Business*—concerned with issues and problems affecting cost of doing business, profitability, efficiency, and good administration.

D. *Marketing*—concerned with external relations, presentation, packaging, sales, reaction of consumers, public, and regulative bodies; service and response key values; advertisement and written word, speeches, and appearances are key mechanisms.

E. *People*—concerned with influencing, selling, training, counseling; effective recruiting, placement, use, motivation, and development of human resources are important; issues of productivity and satisfaction are critical.

5. Which stage of activity do you prefer?

A. *Embryonic*—the very beginning of the life of an organization, everybody wears many hats; everybody pitches in.

B. *Growth*—the enterprise or activity is established but needs better organization, systems, controls, and uniformity in products, policies, pricing, and production.

C. *Mature*—the organization is established, so greater stress on management and financial considerations; more deliberate, informed process of change; less results oriented, more political.

6. Which motivates you most in your work—breadth or depth?

A. *Breadth*—focus more on knowing *where* to get answers and advice than on personal expertise; multi-disciplined; frequently both technical and economic in approach, prefer activities such as labor relations, purchasing office products, industrial engineering, general accounting, quality control, and training.

B. *Depth*—in love with specialty; seek to build up personal expertise and new/better ways of applying in-depth knowledge, then uses these skills to solve problems; prefer activities such as corporate taxation, corrosion metallurgy, arbitration, purchasing electronic components, cost accounting, stress testing, and sales training.

7. Which would you prefer as the end result of your effort?

A. *Tangible Object*—product, process, building.

B. *Measurable results*—sales, profits, yields, returns.

C. *Defined Effort*—problems, needs, requirements.

D. *Addition to Knowledge*—publication, discovery, data.

E. *Impact on Others*—response, use, application.

There are some additional, more personal issues you need to understand about yourself that can help you make sounder decisions for or against certain careers, certain jobs, certain employers. Put an X toward whichever end of each line expresses your way of operating when it comes to the following issues:

(Example: Hands on_____ Hands off)

1. *Kind of Boss You Prefer*

A. Hands on_____ Hands off

B. Collaborativ_____ On Your Own

C. Clear Directions_____ Results Only

D. Readily Available_____ Not Available

E. Know Where You Stand_____ Avoids Confrontation

2. *Kind of Subordinates You Prefer*

A. None_____

B. Equals_____ Subordinates

C. Competent_____ Needing Help

D. Team Players_____ Individualistic

E. Yielding_____ Stubborn

F. Brilliant_____ Average

### 3. Some Organizational and Situational Circumstances You Prefer

A. Certainty_____ Ambiguity

B. Pressure_____ Relaxed

C. Willing to Stand Alone_____ Be With Prevailing View

D. Political_____ Results Oriented

E. Endure to the End_____ Reasonable Effort

F. Conservative_____ Risk-taker

G. New_____ Established

H. Be Change Agent_____ Be Responsive Mainly

I. Manage Your Career_____ Go with the Flow

Now look back at the first part of the survey and list on a separate piece of paper the principal choices you made. For example, you might write down Contributor-Staff-Project-Business-Growth-Depth-Measurable Results.

Then put down the preferences you indicated in the second part of the survey adding your own words to clarify your intentions. For example:

- *Boss*—hands off; collaborative at the beginning; reasonably clear directions of what he or she wants; available when I need him or her; know where I stand.

- *Subordinates*—none.

- *Situational Dynamics*—clear and certain requirements and relationships; moderate pressure; don't like to be isolated; results oriented; reasonable effort but go home at five; kind of conservative; like new tasks but not far out; responder; let management manage, but I like to be asked.

## YOUR IDEAL JOB

The next step in determining your career direction is to describe in writing what you can deliver to an employer. An ideal job description helps you move from merely knowing your strengths to understanding and using your motivational pattern as an integral system. As we have stressed previously, do not extract one ingredient and say it is representative of you; only in the context of the entire pattern can one part be understood properly.

*The purpose of your ideal job description is to summarize your strengths in a single statement.* First, retrieve the elements of your motivational ingredients that you discussed in Chapter 8. Below is one approach you can use to pull the pieces of your pattern together.

*To fulfill my motivational pattern, I need* (Insert your subject matter items—for example, people, ideas, numbers, structural objects.)

*and require my abilities to* (Insert your motivated abilities—for example, observe closely, analyze, negotiate.)

*and which has the end result of* (Insert your central motivational result—for example, a finished product, chance for advancement, greater responsibility, recognition for my contribution.)

This is a writing assignment, so dust off your composition skills. In fleshing out this format, use whatever words communicate your strengths and make it flow. After completing this stage of your job description, it should resemble the following examples.

A job working with people, merchandise, and money; where the condition are not too structured, allowing me to tackle and solve problems that come up and requiring a cool head in the face of a lot of pressure. I need to operate on my own, using my abilities to evaluate people, make friends, sell them on myself and my product, keep my merchandise orderly, and carefully account for my sales and cost of sales. The end result of my work should be an opportunity to participate in the ownership and profits of the business.

You may want to include more details as in the next example.

My ideal job involves research to discover processes, materials, or devices that promise to be distinctive or unusual. The work should provide me with a sense of progression into new areas and with the knowledge that I can be successful by tilling ground that others thought was barren. Competition or a challenge enhances my performance, and the job should require my ability to get results quickly and efficiently. Another aspect of the work should include perfecting the methods of application of the product.

The work should focus on what can be observed or quantified. It should use my gift for identifying and measuring the nature and function of phenomena. I want my results to have practical application no matter how complex or novel the research process.

I should have a leadership role within the organization but my job should provide plenty of flexibility for mixing independent research and administrative duties. The job should require me to supervise persons who possess levels of ability and initiative and who will flourish under loose administrative control.

Remember that you are writing your description of your ideal job; the likelihood is small you will find a position engaging every element of your pattern. However, a concise statement will aid you in your search for a fulfilling career. Integrating the ingredients of your motivational pattern through this exercise gives you an effective tool for remembering and communicating your strengths to others and provides a standard against which you can evaluate a particular job fit.

## Anchor Your Ideal Job Description Within An Industry

To complete your ideal job description, you need to insert references to specific industries or businesses. "A job in sales or customer service for a *retail business selling clothing or home furnishings,* working with people..."

You should screen potential employers from the geographical area in which you plan to settle to narrow your description. We've found the most effective procedure to accomplish this is to put each ingredient from your motivational pattern through the type of sorting process you used earlier to discover the career implications of your pattern.

The first sort is based on the subject matter items with which you are motivated to work. Take your most general subject matter item and identify every industry, business, organization, or profession in which that item is the central focus. If *hardware and equipment* are your screening elements, your list of possibilities after the initial sort might include a foundry; a car dealership; manufacturers of screws, electronic instruments, or pneumatic devices; manufacturers' representatives of plumbing supplies, pumps, or farm implements; the construction and maintenance department of the municipal government; dealers in air conditioning, heating equipment, or office machinery; a trucking firm; a business servicing appliances; or a machine tool shop.

Next, screen the possible employers you have just listed using an element from your motivating circumstances. If that happens to be *potential for sharing profits,* you would eliminate any large organizations or governmental departments in which opportunities for a entrepreneurial spirit don't exist. Unless you want a few years of experience, you will probably eliminate family-owned businesses in which relatives hold all the key positions.

While you are still considering your motivating circumstances examine the contexts that stimulate you. For example, the element of *new or novel situations* may be of importance. The organizations that survived the previous cuts should now be sorted on the basis of whether or not the product involves a new or novel aspect. On this basis, you might retain automobile sales and service but exclude the trucking firm, include the manufacturer of electronic instruments but reject the screw manufacturer, and keep appliance servicing but rule out the plumbing supply house.

If you continue screening in this fashion using the elements from your motivational pattern, you should be able to eliminate many inappropriate jobs.

Once you have identified likely organizations you can consider jobs within them.

If you have diligently done all the exercises that were presented up to this point, you should now possess a substantial amount of data about your strengths and their career implications. You should be reasonably well prepared to identify career problems and search out likely employers. The next step is to look at specific job possibilities.

# CHAPTER TWELVE

# Creating a Job Motivational Pattern

A T THIS POINT you should have narrowed your choices to several potential careers, based on an understanding of your gifts and motivations and expressed in your ideal job description. Your next task is to gather information from potential employers about job opportunities within these careers and to create a motivational pattern for the job, you will later compare to your own pattern.

First, look for sources that can provide you with information on jobs that interest you. For example, you might obtain an official job description or talk to a supervisor or person who has held the job. Once you have gathered this information, try to identify the key components of the work—what we call the *critical requirements*. Then ask for clarification of the terms used in stating those requirements. Because commonly used words can be interpreted to mean extremely different things, you will need to conduct what we call a critical requirements interview to get an accurate picture of what you would actually do on the job. To demonstrate the necessity of the interview, let us take a look at the diverse meanings the word "research" can have when being used to describe a key component of a job.

1. *Research:* experimental, theoretical, long-term objectives, unstructured environment, and delayed payoff.

2. *Research:* applications oriented, working out bugs, considering the market, establishing feasibility in terms of product cost, pressured environment, and short-term payoffs.

3. *Research:* analyzing and trouble-shooting at the production stage, investigating why things don't work, high-pressure environment, and results needed immediately.

## CONDUCTING A CRITICAL REQUIREMENTS INTERVIEW

The goal of your discussion with the job expert is to identify and precisely define critical requirement of the work. to determine a job's vital aspects, consider asking the types of questions that follow:

- Could you tell me what I have to do well to be successful in this job?
- What qualities and skills are critical to successful performance in this job?
- What are the make-or-break demands from this job?

Always ask for examples to illustrate a generalized or abstract response. A method that works well is to concentrate on action verbs. Whenever an action verb such as "organize" is mentioned, consider it to be a door-opener. Ask what's involved in organizing for an example of organizing, how you go about organizing, or how a successful employee in that position would go about organizing.

Whenever an action verb is used, note it and *keep probing until you are satisfied you could describe to someone else what's really involved in the job.* Take notes or, better yet, tape the interview and listen to it later, copying down the salient elements of the job. To help you understand the process of information probing, examine the following dialogue between an interviewer and a person who knows the job's critical requirements.

JOB EXPERT: The person who has this job should be able to plan.

INTERVIEWER: Would you expand on that?

JE: Well, once an assignment is given, he or she has to be able to plan how the job will be done.

I: Would you give me an example of such an assignment and specific actions the person needs to take?

JE: Sure. When the processing unit was moved from the warehouse to the headquarters building, the head of this section had to coordinate the details of the entire move.

I: And what was involved in that?

JE: He spent a lot of time with supervisors from the processing unit getting the data needed to make the move.

I: What kind of data?

JE: The quantity and size of each type of equipment, the number of desks and chairs, the layout of the new space, the workload they had to meet during the week of the move. Everything in the processing unit had to be listed, transported, and put in the right place.

I: And what did he do with this data?

JE: He developed a flow chart outlining all the steps that had to be taken prior to the week of moving and clearly indicated who was responsible for having things accomplished by specific times.

I: Could you give me an example of some of those steps?

JE: Yes. Well, the processing unit had ordered new equipment to replace some old pieces and to add new capability; the delivery and testing of that equipment at least a month before the move was essential. Four weeks prior to the move, the person coordinating it worked under a lot of pressure. The group that originally occupied the processing unit's new space had to be moved out, then the carpenters and electricians shifted around work compartments and wiring. And painters were brought in to make repairs and change the color scheme.

Meanwhile, delivery of the new equipment began. Our coordinator had to organize all those events and stay on top of the changes that inevitably occurred.

The interview proceeds in this manner until the interviewer uncovers all the job's critical requirements. If you feel you need more structure to conduct a critical requirements interview, we have created the following series of questions to guide you.

## CRITICAL REQUIREMENTS INTERVIEW QUESTIONNAIRE

JOB TITLE/DEPARTMENT:

*Door Openers*

1. Could you tell me what you do in one or two sentences?
2. What are the specific duties for which you are held accountable?
3. Could you describe for me your "typical" day?

*Pinning Down*

4. Can you give me examples of...(refer to the areas mentioned in the answers to 1,2,and 3 above)
5. What do you mean by directing? developing? problem solving? implementing? administering?
6. What factors are critical to successful performance in your job?
7. How structured is your job?
8. How high is the level of stress in this job?
9. How much recognition do you receive for doing your job?
10. What role does your supervisor play?
11. What interaction is there with co-workers?
12. What kinds of resources are available?

*Wrapping Up*

13. What provides you with the most satisfaction in your job?
14. What causes you the most frustration?
15. How do you measure the results of your work?

The next step is to summarize the data you have collected. Summaries prepared by two different individuals are presented for your guidance. Use these formats, or one of your own design, to capture the essence of the position for which you are preparing the job pattern.

## Example 1: Market Analyst—Market Services Division

WHAT

Conducts contract marketing studies, marketing opportunity studies, pricing strategies, and feasibility studies of new products/materials. Works on three to four projects at a time.

HOW

Stages of a project: determines objectives, outlines project, establishes timetable and production plan, analyzes costs, and delivers project presentation.

SKILLS AND PERSONAL QUALITIES

Skills required: organizing, developing interpersonal relationships, speaking in front of groups, negotiating over the phone, analyzing profits and costs, determining objectives and goals, meeting deadlines, assertiveness without a support system, and self-motivation.

SATISFACTION

When I discover profitable business opportunities for the company.

FRUSTRATION

Working with product groups is difficult—considerable amount of their time is needed, but they feel one meeting should be enough. Many times nothing comes of my marketing recommendations and after the presentation, the decision is out of my control.

ORGANIZATION

The job is highly visible and loosely organized. You are your own boss.

## Example 2: Development Planner—Research and Development

A person working with this group is one of ten to thirteen professionals reporting to a Research and Development supervisor. Because this group interacts heavily with the manufacturing operation and personnel, the environment blends a long-range focus with a sharp awareness of day-to-day business needs. A development planner carries out one or more projects. The job applies principles of science and engineering to solve current business needs. Improving the company's position requires determining whether existing technology can be applied or if new technology must be developed. Large scale projects may take three to five or more years to complete; the smaller projects can be completed in six months to two years.

Assessing the feasibility of technology is the heart of the work. Because the company is in the private sector, the development planner must always keep cost effectiveness in mind; the person can be successful only if he or she incorporates a business perspective into the research.

A typical project sequence involves the following:

- Identify business needs.
- Identify and evaluate alternatives to meet these needs by changing equipment, processes, or procedures.
- Choose an alternative and determine if existing technology is applicable or if equipment or processes must be developed.
- Develop plans to implement improvements; communicate and collaborate with others within the company who are studying similar possibilities.
- Sell the proposal to supervisor and other necessary parties.
- Carry out plans by coordinating specialized design and construction groups as well as individual contribution.
- Analyze the improvements' success and modify as necessary. Re-evaluate business needs to determine if more work is justified.

## DRAWING OUT PATTERN ELEMENTS

The next step is to extract the key motivational elements from your summary of the job's critical requirements. The key elements will correspond to the ingredients of motivational patterns. Therefore you should arrange the key component groups in the following order: circumstances, necessary abilities, and required operating relationship. For instance, in the market analyst example, we've identified the critical requirements that follow.

*Subject Matter*

- money
- people
- materials
- markets
- strategies

*Circumstances*

- deadlines
- visibility
- projects
- potential for profit

- unstructured environment

*Abilities*

- investigating by interviewing
- planning by setting objectives
- evaluating by analyzing
- influencing by presenting and advocating
- organizing by integrating detail
- communicating by verbal discussion and written

*Operating Relationships*

- individualist

From the summary for the development planner we've BT extracted these key components:

*Subject Matter*

- principles
- processes
- technical
- equipment
- details
- methods

*Circumstances*

- needs
- potential for improvement

*Abilities*

- learning by participating
- evaluating by analyzing
- planning by strategizing
- influencing by persuading
- developing by adapting
- overseeing by monitoring

*Operating Relationship*

- coordinator

Using this simple format, extract the key elements from your critical requirements interview notes and develop a motivational pattern for that job.

When you have finished, briefly describe the essence of each key element. Here are examples of how some elements could be described:

- *Sales/Marketing* (under subject matter)
  Should have a major interest in sales and in the mechanics involved when making sales. Should view events and problems in terms of their impact on sales. Should be sensitive to situations that could to sales.

- *Problems* (under circumstances)
  Should spend considerable energy anticipating, preventing, or solving problems. Should be responsive to weak points that could be potential sources of trouble.

- *Plan/Anticipate* (under abilities)
  Should be able to focus on what will happen a year or two in the future. Should understand the long-term implications of current problems, needs, trends, data, and shifts in demand.

- *Coordinator* (under operating relationship)
  Should be skilled at motivating others to use their talents to accomplish goals. Should function as a coordinator for projects integrating several functions.

Once you have completed the exercises in this chapter, you've identified the critical requirements of a particular job. Knowing the key components is the only way to evaluate, without actually working in the job, whether you will be fulfilled by the work. Now that you have the vital information about your motivational requirements and those of the job in which you are interested, the next step is to compare your pattern with the job's pattern. This process is described in detail in the next chapter.

## CHAPTER THIRTEEN
# Finding the Right Job For You

YOU HAVE NOW gathered the data necessary to compare what you require from a job to what a particular job requires from you. Each element of your motivational pattern's ingredients must be evaluated against the critical requirements of the job(s) being considered.

For ease of comparison, we are listing the motivational ingredients in the same sequence used previously: subject matter, circumstances, abilities, and operating relationships. As noted when we discussed the career implications of your pattern (Chapter 10), your central motivational result is not an efficient point for comparison; most jobs accommodate a variety of results. However, after comparing the elements of the other four ingredients and determining that the job it is promising, it is essential to evaluate the job in light of your one desired result.

Whether or not the job will allow you to do unique work, have an impact on the organization, develop new systems, gain a response from customers, satisfy the requirements of the line organizion, or whatever your central motivational result might be, should be clear when you examine the job's key components with your desired payoff in mind. Will this job fulfill your central motivational result? If it does not, look elsewhere regardless of how closely your other motivational ingredients match the job's critical requirements.

The following example compares a client's pattern to an actual job pattern. A word of explanation about the format is required. Opposite each element in the job pattern we have presented the corresponding element from our client's pattern. When no exactly matching element is found in the individual's pattern, the material may explain how other elements can act as substitutes for the missing requirement.

## JOB MATCH

(District Operations Manager)

| JOB'S MOTIVATIONAL PATTERN | PERSON'S MOTIVATIONAL PATTERN |
|---|---|

**Subject Matter**

*Sales/Marketing*

*No Corresponding Element*

Should have a major interest in sales and in the mechanics involved when making sales. Should view events and problems in terms of their impact on sales. Should be sensitive to situations that could head to sales.

Although sales and marketing are not elements of my pattern, I can focus on sales targets if specified as a job requirement. Without such a requirement, I would not be sensitive to circumstances or opportunities that have an effect on sales or be particularly excited by marketing strategies and techniques. I would track sales if it was a required goal and do my best to meet that requirement.

*Systems*

*Systems*

Should be disposed to work through systems, particularly to coordinate interlocking work. Should concentrate on improving systems or having systems built where a need exists.

I am able to handle the logistics of complex operations. Although I will work with others to design and install a system to meet requirements, I would not tend to systematize before the need surfaced.

**Circumstances**

*Potential for Profit*

*Measurable Results*

Should be concerned about making money for the company. Should be in tune with what increases or decreases profit.

I am tuned to making money and obtaining quantifiable results. To the extend that making profit is a requirement or goal, I would spend significant effort trying to meet it.

*Self Environment*

*Standards*

Should be concerned about the technical integrity of the facilities, piping, and equipment; the safety of customers and workers; and with safety's impact on management decisions about work load, quality of personnel, and materials.

Should spend considerable energy anticipating, preventing, or solving problems. Should be responsive to weak points that could be potential sources of trouble.

| Problems | Needs |
|---|---|
| Should spend considerable energy anticipating, preventing, or solving problems. Should be responsive to weak points that could be potential sources of trouble. | I would be highly responsive to problems when expressed as needs requiring resolution and when my role was clear to me. |

## Abilities

| *Interview/Inquire* | *Interview/Inquire* |
|---|---|
| Should be able to get at essential facts and critical issues of a situation that involves either a technical or personnel problem. | I am good at asking questions to get the information needed on a subject matter of motivating value. |
| *Prioritize* | *Prioritize* |
| Should be skilled at evaluating changing circumstances and establishing priorities to achieve critical objectives with available resources. Should be able to separate what is critical from what is desirable. Should be able to focus on operational goals and skilled at evaluating a prospect in terms of profitability. | As long as I have adequate standards and guidelines, I would be able to evaluate the impact of circumstances and data on current goals. In order to evaluate I require an established standard to compare the new situation against. |
| *Plan/Anticipate* | *No Corresponding Element* |
| Should be able to focus on what will happen a year or two in the future. Should understand the long-term implications of current problems, needs, trends, data, and shifts in demand. Should be able to allocate available resources toward future plans. | My ability to anticipate requires having experienced something similar and comparing the situations. |

## Operating Relationship

| *Manager* | *Manager* |
|---|---|
| Should be skilled at motivating others to use their talents to accomplish goals. Should function as a coordinator for projects integrating several functions. | I have some managerial abilities and am particularly strong as a liaison person for project management. My management performance would improve if I could select my own team or weed out those who don't fit. |

What do you think of the match between the critical requirements of the job and the motivational pattern of the person? Should the job be offered and accepted? Although only some of the elements matched, our belief is that the job fit is acceptable. However, because the match is not outstanding, both parties need to be aware that the person would require considerable support in the sales/marketing aspects of the job and in anticipating future situations.

Your job is to follow the format indicated; define the pattern elements required by the job and compare them with your pattern elements. Finally, of course, you need to evaluate the comparison.

## IMPROVING YOUR CURRENT JOB FIT

Throughout this book, we have advised you to select and remain in a vocation that engages your gifts and your heart. The phrase *and remain* is intended to be a shout. Don't leave a job that you enjoy just because you can climb "higher." Here's a typical scenario. Most people are only "average" in their performance because they are not gifted at their jobs. If you're good at what you do, you will stand out and will be offered a position at a higher level, probably as a supervisor. Management doesn't always do the right thing; they may promote a person who is good at his or her current job without considering what the new position may require. Don't let them make that mistake with you! *Before changing titles, make sure the next job fits you as well or better than your present one*. Advances that frequently result in job mismatch are:

- from a contributor's role to a manager's position.
- from a position in the field to a position at headquarters.
- from supervising people in your own field to supervising a variety of specialists.
- from supervising one location to supervising many locations.
- from running one project to overseeing a variety of projects.
- from handling one product line to handling several diversified products.
- from working with a compatible boss to working with one who manages in a different style.
- from a position where you follow instructions to a position where you make most of the decisions.
- from a team member position to a field position operating alone.

The most rewarding career choice for a person's immediate future may be to continue to develop in the present job. To help you do that, we would like you to analyze your current position by answering the following questions.

1. What critical requirements of your present job make substantial use of your strengths (for example: handle difficult problems in a limited time frame; anticipate overload work schedules; come up with design concepts)?

2. What critical requirements of your present job clearly fall outside your strengths (for example, handle customers poorly; don't take action until problems become serious; do little planning)?

3. What duties could be eliminated or transferred to another employee to improve your job match?

4. What duties could be added to your job that would make greater use of your strengths?

5. What could your supervisor provide that would help you improve your job performance?

To help you understand the sort of things your supervisor could do to give you help, examine the following list of issues in the light of your motivational pattern. Do you need clearer directions, less control, an opportunity to participate in decisions affecting you, or something else?

- Controls—either loosen or tighten them
- Structure—clarity or make fluid
- Standards—establish objectives and express expectations
- Goals—express in terms meaningful to employee
- Visibility—build it into or remove it from the job
- Jurisdiction—make clear boundaries or leave open to successful aggression
- Administrative Detail—people share or people specialize
- Feedback—provide direct contact with field or customer or insulate from people
- Decision Making—delegate, share, or eliminate it
- Participation—collaborate, support, or command
- Systems—set up as substitute for missing ability

## Tips to Improve Job Fit

Depending on the flexibility of your work place, you might consider bringing any of the following suggestions to your supervisor, as a way to improve your job fit and build career muscle through your current job. Write out the specific suggestions you might make. Examples of solutions are provided in parentheses.

Horizontal Expansion (I want the entire responsibility for dealing with customers.)
Solution:

Vertical Expansion (I would like to prepare the progress reports requested by division management.)
Solution:

Project Assignments (I want to be part of the team that develops and spearheads new programs.)
Solution:

Collateral Assignments (I would enjoy assisting with the instruction of new employees.)
Solution:

Increases Authority (I want the authority to approve payment schedules of up to three months.)
Solution:

Clarify Responsibility (I expect to be held responsible for meeting new standards.)
Solution:

Provide Feedback (I want to have a continuing dialogue with field services personnel.)
Solution:

Eliminate Duties (I would like all follow-up responsibilities removed.)
Solution:

## Coping Strategies

Finally, let us suggest some ways to handle those duties that require strengths you don't have. First, look to the strengths of those around you: peers, subordinates, even your supervisor. Ask for help!

If you were behind the door when they passed out the planning marbles, ask someone good at planning to help you. If you have a tough time making hard decisions, ask someone good at decision-making to help (even the people working for you!). When you are dealing with duties you do moderately well but are not motivated to do, set up iron bound rules that you are not allowed to violate—for example, if you hate writing letters, tell yourself that you are going to lock yourself up for one hour every day and get the job done, perhaps allowing yourself a goodie of some sort upon completion of the task. Read some of the many self-help books written by behavioral psychologists and you'll get many tips on improving your performance in those areas difficult for you. Just don't get confused about who you are!

# CHAPTER FOURTEEN

# The Real You

PEOPLE become confused when we emphasize the consistency of motivational patterns. They have seen others become increasingly skillful through practice, they know people who have disciplined their personal lives and become happier, they have observed underdogs become successful, and watched stockbrokers leave the city to become farmers. Surely each of these individuals changed.

We do agree that people tend to use their gifts more effectively with maturity. The stability to which we refer pertains to the number of motivated abilities a person possesses when born. In our work we have not seen an individual acquire motivated abilities in addition to those displayed early in life.

Let us compare your motivational pattern to your physique. Your basic physical characteristics are predetermined. If you were born white, you will never be black; if you were born brown-eyed, you will never be blue-eyed; if you are 20 years old and still short, you will never be tall. However you can change sloppy posture and can exercise to keep trim. The 98-pound weakling can change; he or she doesn't become a different person but becomes more of what he or she is already.

Woven into the lives of people who are otherwise well suited for their jobs are numerous potential obstacles that may stand between them and abundant life. Many people have poor work habits, compulsive personal habits, abrasive mannerisms, emotional problems, physical ailments or a fear of them, domestic strife, non-social behavior, difficulties resulting from past behavior, inadequate training or formal education, areas lacking discipline, fears, or anger.

Personal obstacles, as well as societal or environmental ones, can prevent a person from feeling the contentment that could be derived from a fitting career. We are not trying to solve all the difficulties that plague mankind; but we can urge people to address unhealthy attitudes of the mind and spirit. Someone is gifted at dealing with your problems and with the help of others you will find that person. Don't settle for internal ugliness just because it's familiar. We encourage you to remain hopeful because we have seen many troubled individuals achieve internal health.

## A LIFE-PERVADING PATTERN

We want to repeat that knowing your motivational pattern does not mean you know everything about yourself. Character or temperament are not described;

nor does your pattern reveal your fears or psychological preoccupations although it may trigger them. When you examine details from your life, you will be amazed at how they mirror your motivational pattern. Many negative emotions are triggered when your pattern is crossed or blocked and you are unable to use your abilities. For example, if you are motivated to get results, side issues will probably be irritating, and people who get in the way may be an aggravation.

If you are motivated to plan carefully, you may become anxious when circumstances require you to wing it. And if you are motivated to keep people happy, confrontation will very likely make you uneasy.

Since much behavior is motivational, understanding the specifics of your motivational pattern is enormously valuable. This self-knowledge gives you the closest thing you will ever have to objectivity about your behavior.

Coping with emotional responses to motivational frustration is easier if you realize the source of the frustration. This understanding is the key to effectively managing situations in which you find yourself; whether you respond, how you respond, the position you take, and the role you seek. To gain greater insight into motivational behavior, take a look at your past behavior; look for evidence of a consistent pattern. Here are some exercises to assist you.

1. *Confronting A Need*

Remember a time when you were confronted by someone with a need. Describe how you reacted.

Did you

dig into your pocket?

go back to reading the newspaper?

give advice?

walk in the opposite direction?

other?

What elements of your motivational pattern influenced your action?

2. *Making A Decision*

Recall and describe a situation when you had to make an important decision.

Did you

gather pertinent facts first?

make a decision without deliberation?

consider the details repeatedly?

procrastinate as long as possible?

identify several reasons that would prevent you from deciding?
other?
What elements of your motivational pattern influenced your action?

### 3. *Meeting A Challenge*

Consider a situation in which you were challenged. Describe it briefly.
Did you
fight back?
retreat to think it over?
seek a compromise?
quickly build your defense?
other?
What elements of your motivational pattern influenced your action?

### 4. *Disciplining A Child*

Recall and describe the last time you had to firmly discipline a child.
Did you
reason with the child?
count to ten, then talk?
avoid the problem?
accept any excuse?
other?
What elements of your motivational pattern influenced your action?

If you would like more insight into how your motivational pattern pervades life, consider the following points. Examine your response to see how your sadness, elation, or antagonism reflects the relationship between your pattern and the world.

1. Describe the details of a situation in which you felt angry or frustrated. What were you trying to do? What happened and how did you feel? Do elements of your motivational pattern explain why?

2. Do the same as in 1, using a situation in which you felt bored, anxious, elated, or depressed.

3. Describe the connections between your pattern and
what you think about when you wake up
how you handle money

what you do in your spare time

how you handle yourself in a social situation with strangers

what kind of car you have and how you drive

how you order (or prepare) and eat a meal

what kind of clothes you wear and how you approach buying them

what you fantasize about

how you maintain your possessions

what you pray about

the nature of your criticism about people and issues in your life

how you function in a familiar group

the strong views you have about any public issues

The causes or issues that tap our passion reflect our motivational pattern. Realizing the self-serving quality of our commitments is the first step to maturity. People who help the underdog, work with troubled individuals, and embolden the minorities may consider their purpose selfless. It may be helping others, but they should not deceive themselves about their motivation. Self-fulfillment is their primary goal though they may *not* be aware of it. Those dedicated to changing people or changing the system are dedicated because they feed themselves through causing change. The crusader tears down institutions or customs that he or she believes cause injustice. This person may possess the motivated ability to clear the way, but not the ability to build up. Depending on how you perceive the cause, and remember your view is colored by your motivational pattern, the crusader will be considered a hero or an outlaw.

Given any philosophy, rules of behavior, theology, or set of customs, you must expect your motivational pattern to edit your personal values. Generally, we react positively to situations that engage our patterns and negatively to those which block them, and the emphasis we place on these situations is also affected by our pattern. An individual motivated to fulfill needs and requirements is likely to comply with the demands of a set of requirements; the person motivated to be unique will choose any path other than the one well used. Our patterns determine if we are motivated to work within or outside the established system. Warring motivational intentions permeate all human activity. A tendency to overlook what is best for the situation in order to follow personal motivations is true for both neighborhood kids playing in the sandbox and our government officials. For example, consider a woman who is both a mother and a manager. She attends lectures on management and understands she should delegate responsibility, but she will also continue to control her subordinates and children closely if motivated to do so. She can try to apply her learned skills, but through the pretext of better communication, performance review sessions, or problems-of-the-week conferences, she will end up with her hands back on the wheel. If direct attempts fail, she will find subtle ways of maintaining control.

As another example, a man motivated to operate as an individualist will find some way of functioning as one whether he is in the role of engineer, husband, minister, or linebacker. If someone attempts to get this individualist to be part of a team, he will seek tasks that he can perform without being harnessed to others and which will reflect the results of his individual efforts. When this person is made manager because of his success, he may end up trying to do all the important work himself, using others as his extensions; or abdicating all management responsibility and attacking a project he can work on alone.

# CHAPTER FIFTEEN

# Defining Relationships

TO ENHANCE your understanding of relationships remember that each of us speaks from the perspective of our motivational pattern. Our perception is narrowed by our motivations; we need to back away from our unique view to give room to other ways of perceiving and operating. Conflicts that appear to be based on principles may be merely a collision of motivational patterns. This realization should illuminate many of the problems in your relationships and provide a basis for better communication and ways of operating with others in the future.

To strengthen your grasp of your motivational pattern's expression in typical job and family situations, we have devised some fictional motivational patterns. Take on a detective role to analyze the information and describe the relationships that you feel would develop. Assume that no psychological, temperament, or cultural factors exist to complicate the issues.

## ANALYZING BUSINESS RELATIONSHIPS

Let us first look at a work situation. Here, we will focus on an employee's relationship with a boss. On the next page are the motivational pattern elements with which you will work:

| Person | Central Motivational Result | Operating Relationship | Subject Matter | Motivating Circumstances | Motivated Abilities |
|---|---|---|---|---|---|
| Employee | innovate (pioneer) | individualist independent of authority | principles concepts technical | fluid potential for growth new visibility | conceive experiment analyze teach |
| Boss A | master (perfect) | director | details hardware money | structured goals efficiency | analyze plan develop procedures control |
| Boss B | exploit potential | manager | technical ideas details money | goals effectiveness parameters | investigate develop conceive facilitate coach |

After comparing the employee's motivational pattern with that of each boss type, try to determine any problems that might develop. Use these questions to help you complete the exercise:

1. When the employee and the boss look at the results of the employee's work, what does each focus on and find most satisfying? How do these focuses compare?

2. What measuring sticks will the boss use to judge the employee's work? What are the employee's measuring sticks? How do the measuring sticks compare?

3. How will the boss manage? What does the employee need from a manager to work effectively? How do the styles of management compare?

## Our Analysis of Boss A

Let us share our analysis. If the employee had asked the right questions before taking this job, he or she would have discovered that Boss A wants to manicure, while the employee wants to experiment. The employee likes to work on the big picture and may resent the detailed work that the boss expects. The things about which the two might argue include: the tight budget the boss insists the employee work within; the boss's concern with procedural documentation so others can reproduce the employee's work; and the boss's desire to direct the employee's research methods, even though the boss doesn't fully understand the principles the employee is following.

We see no way of turning this into an effective working relationship. Both people could continue to make friendly attempts to improve the situation but the individual motivational patterns naturally clash. The employee should change jobs because neither his or her pattern nor the boss's is going to change.

## Our Analysis of Boss B

If the employee asked Boss B the right questions during the job interview, he or she could have made a calculated guess that the two of them would work well together. Boss B would have an interest in accommodating the employee's way of working. The boss would see the employee's innovativeness and pioneering as exciting possibilities; would know to give the employee plenty of room to operate; would like the employee's ability to determine the direction to pursue new potential; and would encourage the employee to give presentations about his or her work to management. Although Boss B might have some uneasiness as to whether or not the employee would keep in mind agreed upon objectives and make serious attempts to try to meet them, the boss would know when the employee reached critical points and would encourage him or her to focus on a feasible solution.

## Avoiding Bad Working Relationships

Determining how your potential manager will actually operate is always a gamble. Many people have found too many people to be different from the characters they first encountered to feel confident in their evaluation of a supervisor. Rather than leave yourself open for surprises, we suggest you stack the deck in your favor. Ask questions before you agree to take the job; this is the best time to investigate what the job will hold.

To get an idea of the supervisor's management style ask: "How do you like to manage those who report to you?" Some supervisors may give textbooks answers; others may tell you what they think they should be doing. A supervisor might say that he or she likes to give people freedom to operate in their own style, wants people to know exactly what is expected, lets people discover what needs to be done, checks with employees every day to make sure everything is going well, or likes working closely with people. The supervisor's answer may be based on either his or her motivational pattern or what he or she thinks his or her job requires. To discover the source of the answer ask the supervisor for a couple of examples. You can also confirm the person's management style by talking with his or her subordinates or co-workers. The management fit is only one factor among many when you assess job fit, but it is an important one that most applicants ignore.

## ANALYZING FAMILY RELATIONSHIPS

This book does not intend to deal with the complexities of interpersonal relationships; but we can offer some suggestions that have proven helpful in managing motivational differences.

### *Relating to a Partner*

If you are single, the information in this section may give you an advantage in finding a partner with whom you will find contentment. Complementary motivational patterns are not tickets to marital bliss; but we know from our counseling experience that awareness of both partners' patterns enhances the likelihood of compatibility considerably. This knowledge may also provide a way to head off or defuse conflicts that may occur. To help you practice analyzing a relationship, we will give you fictional motivational patterns for two people, similar to the patterns we used when analyzing relationships with potential bosses. As before you should try to describe the relationship you feel would develop.

| Person | Central Motivational Result | Operating Relationship | Subject Matter | Motivating Circumstances | Motivated Abilities |
|--------|------------------|------------|--------|---------------|-----------|
| Partner A | innovate (pioneer) | individualist independent of authority | concepts technical principles | fluid potential for growth visibility new | conceive experiment analyze teach |
| Partner B | gain response | team member | people relationships art | unique status finished product | study draw/design counsel execute |

OUR ANALYSIS

This appears to be a good match of motivational patterns and should lead to a successful relationship. When difficulties do arise, Partner B would probably take the initiative to work out the differences and is open to Partner A's response and involvement in solving problems. Though the two do not have similar subject matter, they can find activities in which both can function as a team, though activities in which they can both participate but take individual roles would be best. For example, if Partner B proposes a new furniture arrangement, both could experiment with it until both liked it. Or if both decide that the yard needs landscaping, they should work together to figure out their respective roles; Partner A might generate the ideas and then talk them over with Partner B, who would do the drawings and researches the plant selection. For recreation, both partners should consider playing an individualist sport or hobby together like golf, skiing, or chess. Each can enjoy demonstrating individual competence yet share in the fun.

## Relating to a Child

An understanding of motivational patterns and relationships is central to being an effective parent. The major problem we have seen in our many counseling sessions with young people hinges on the principle with which we began this book: *Each person is already designed.* Many parents feel they must make their children succeed and supply the definition of success. These attempts are not only futile but can distort the child's direction. We have found that it is not unusual for parents to give or withhold love to achieve the desired results. The clever parent does so in a way that prevents people outside the family from noticing and is often unaware of what he or she is doing. Parents whose own motivational patterns include *controlling*, *directing*, or *managing* may be especially prone to this type of manipulation.

Parents chose to control or confirm their child's direction. When dealing with obedience, we feel it is acceptable to use the word *control*; but in the context of life ambitions, wise parents recognize their child's unique characteristics and learn to *confirm* rather than to control or change the direction that already exists. To confirm, parents replace their aspirations with the intention of discovering what is fulfilling to the child and nurturing the child's development.

This approach admits considerable freedom; the responsibility of determining the child's future is replaced by the exciting discovery of the child's unique design. As the child discovers him or her self, he or she must learn to appreciate the characteristics that present themselves. Parents' attitudes are the primary influence on a child's feelings of self-worth. For children to learn to appreciate their gifts and motivations, their parents must act as role models, showing respect and appreciation for their own gifts. Some parents are confused when they discover a child has low self-esteem in spite of all the affirmations they have given. In many instances, the child senses the parents' standard of self-evaluation rather than hearing what the parent says about the child's gifts. The parent who makes conscious attempts not to impose perfectionist standards on the child, but at the same time is extremely critical of him or herself, imparts a demanding standard that the child may observe.

Parents teach best what they have experienced. When they have identified their own gifts, they can sincerely express their gratitude for specific life experiences; they provide a potent example for their children to follow in learning to be joyful about being themselves. "Practice what you preach" certainly holds true in relationships with children. The healthiest attitude parents can bring to family life is enthusiasm for the individual traits of family members. If your children sense that you genuinely support them, the inevitable mistakes you will make as a parent can be of much less consequence. Once again we will present some fictional motivational patterns for you to evaluate.

Compare the motivational operating methods of each child with the pattern for the parent and answer the questions that follow.

| Person | Central Motivational Result | Operating Relationship | Subject Matter | Motivating Circumstances | Motivated Abilities |
|--------|------------------|------------|---------|-------------|-----------|
| Parent | innovate (pioneer) | individualist independent of authority | concepts principles | fluid potential for growth mobility | conceive experiment analyze teach |
| Child A | make the grade | team member | group activity projects programs presentations | difficulties requirements time available | practice persevere plan execute perform |
| Child B | serve | individualist | values people | causes needs potential for development | learn conceptualize write speak advocate |

1. With which child's motivational pattern is the parent most compatible?

2. Which child is more likely to spend time with the parent? How does the parent react to each child? Which child needs people?

3. With which child is the parent most likely to argue?

4. Which child's brings home the injured cats and stray dogs and the underdogs from school?

5. How does each child deal with school work?

OUR ANALYSIS

The parent is more compatible with Child A because both are individualists and also tend to communicate their ideas. They give each other room to operate;

but of the two of them, the child is more likely to initiate conversation, especially when he or she observes that the parent needs help with something.

If Child B wasn't a relation, he or she is the type of person who would both the parent. Child B wants to do things with others and attempts to get family members involved with his or her projects and friends.

All three need other people because humans are social beings; but the function people fulfill differs for each of them according to their unique motivational needs. The parent needs others only occasionally, as an audience. Child A shares this tendency but is also strongly motivated to become involved with people to help them meet their personal needs or for a special cause. Child B needs others as an audience for his or her performances, but in addition the child gathers people into his or her projects as team members.

Arguments are likely to occur between the parent and Child A who will take issue with the parent, especially for another person's sake. Child B has the tendency to seek the parents' approval.

Child A is the child who brings home the dogs and cats. He/she is drawn to all needy creatures and takes action to help.

Child B works hard to get good grades but finds independent assignments trying. Child A's school experience is a bit more uneven. The amount of effort he or she applies is dependent on the subject matter; this child's term papers wow the teachers when he or she is allowed to choose the topic.

Unfortunately, the parent doesn't realize that the child does not have or want life-goals. The child knows that the two live in two different worlds; that the parent's lifestyle is decidedly neat and permanent compared to his or hers. The parent takes care of things; so does the child until they are replaced by others.

## *Relations To Parents*

To enhance your understanding of how to use motivational patterns within the context of family relationships, we will present one final exercise. In the example on the next page, you will examine another relationship between a fictional parent and child.

| Person | Central Motivational Result | Operating Relationship | Subject Matter | Motivating Circumstances | Motivated Abilities |
|--------|------------------------------|-------------------------|----------------|---------------------------|---------------------|
| Child | innovate (pioneer) | individualist independent of authority | concepts principles | fluid potential for growth visibility | conceive experiment analyze teach |
| Parent | acquire (possess) | manager | costs details physical (manual) problems | structured results pressure obstacles | evaluate strategize organize operate |

Compare the listed motivational patterns and then answer the following questions:

1. How do the child and the parent get along?

2. What behavior patterns did the parent criticize when the child was young?

3. What has the parent's reaction been to the child's life-style?

OUR ANALYSIS

Unlike relationships with bosses, whom one can leave if the fit does not work, the relationship with one's parent lasts a lifetime and problems must be resolved for both persons' emotional health. In this example, much work needs to be done to deal with the clash of basic elements in motivational patterns. The child enjoys new experiences and is always on the lookout for something on the horizon. In contrast, the parent intends on keeping the present situation under control. He or she focuses on what exists; the child focuses on what is possible.

As loving and concerned for the child's welfare and success as the parent might be, he or she finds the child's hopeful, conceptual inclinations impractical. The parent is comfortable dealing with concrete results and thinks about what things cost, while the child knows things will "somehow work out." The parent does not understand why the child lives so far away, and the child doesn't tell the parent why he or she needs to get away from the parent's management and do things his or her own way. The child's independence hurts the parent, especially when the parent wants to help the child solve his or her problems. The parent knows the child jumps into things without planning, and would like to assist in translating the child's life goals into practical steps.

YOU

THE OTHER PERSON

| | Fit/Mis-fit | Suggestions |
|---|---|---|
| One Result | | |
| Relation | | |
| Subject Matter | | |
| Circumstances | | |
| Abilities | | |

One Result

Relation

Subject Matter

Circumstances

Abilities

# CHAPTER SIXTEEN

# Implications for Education and Training

WHEN YOU analyzed the fictional children's behavior in the previous chapter, you answered a question about how they applied themselves to school work. We want to mention two important influences on a child's attitude toward school that weren't considered: the first is the strong influence that family values regarding education have on a child's learning and the second is the importance of the role that schools play in the socialization process. Learning takes place both through experience and through formal education. In school, the individual's motivational factors either enhance or block the academic learning process. A child's motivational pattern may be a useful resource for helping parents understand their child's reaction to school.

We believe that compulsive education based on traditional values of Western civilization and tempered with an understanding of today's needs is critical to our culture's survival. Because of education's role, we feel it is reasonable to require all members of our society to meet educational standards, especially those producing literacy.

Regardless of a child's motivational pattern, we and society require the child to study some material that he or she might not choose if the decision were left up to the individual. Society expects large amounts of time be spent in learning activities that may not match an individual's design. We must reconcile the need for standard educational proficiency with the fact that students are motivated to learn only certain subject matter in a specific way to accomplish unique objectives.

A student who competes for grades is not going to be transformed into one who is motivated by a desire to possess knowledge. But if a student works to gain teacher approval, exploiting that tendency to produce the optimum learning situation for the particular student makes sense. If grades were eliminated, we might eliminate any further effort from students motivated by them.

The way students learn has little to do with the prescribed educational system. A student will learn precisely as he or she is designed to learn. Students have the choice of becoming fully engaged in an educational opportunity. However, they are more likely to apply themselves if teachers use the knowledge of each student's motivational elements to encourage the process. Perhaps the time has come for educators to admit that they must recognize a child's unique pattern. The gifted teachers are those who are most willing to act on that truth: they are flexible enough in their teaching approaches to accommodate each student.

Many of those in education are not teachers by motivation. Among our clients we have found that a percentage (as high as 70%) are instead motivated to organize, control, manage, act, or build relationships. We know that people who have been identified as teachers through their achievement activities want real learning to take place and have no intention of using the classroom to do anything else. This is true in private, parochial, or public schools. If you gather into a faculty people whose motivational patterns provide evidence that they are teachers and give them sound objectives, you will have a superb educational system. Too often education is lifeless and of little value when it should be a personally rich and rewarding experience for every student. Instead of being a foundation for a lifetime occupation, academic experience is often irrelevant. A person can complete 16 or more years of education and not understand even the essentials about his or her motivational pattern. The failure to recognize the unique design of each child may be disastrous. If students are not equipped during youth and early adulthood with the self-knowledge necessary to pursue satisfying careers, it is likely that the adult will remain ill equipped and will spend his or her life in a race he or she was never meant to enter.

You should not fall into the trap of equating your identity with the area you have studied; a diploma does not necessarily represent your abilities. The subject matter studied and the grades received are only evidence of strengths in those areas if you were good at and enjoyed what you studied. An individual's education often does not express his or her value to an employer unless in earning the degree or certificate motivated abilities were stimulated.

## CAREERS AND CREDENTIALS

As we just mentioned, college graduates tend to equate themselves with their educations. We recommend that young people consider the possibility of acquiring credentials after thoroughly evaluating their motivational gifts; only then can they direct their education toward fitting careers. If people perceive themselves as active managers of motivated abilities, they can invest their capabilities and focus their energy in a more effective manner. One key to accomplishing significant goals is to develop discipline by making the most of what you have and to be willing to sacrifice short-term benefits for long-term goals.

Because of their motivated abilities, some individuals will be drawn naturally to training. This makes it easier for them to be active managers of their gifts. Others' patterns contain nothing to attract them to education; they must exercise considerable effort to stay on course and fight the constant temptation to cut corners. Many become discouraged during the training situation because they do not realize that the activities do not represent the circumstances involved when actually practicing in the profession. Career goals that match your motivational pattern should not be rejected just because the training requirements do not match your abilities.

Requirements for obtaining credentials can cause mixed reactions from people. Most may agree that credentials are necessary to maintain professional excellence but resent the bureaucracy involved. The stance each of us takes toward regulations varies depending on our motivational elements. People motivated to overcome and prevail are tempted to crusade against requirements; those motivated to fulfill needs and requirements eagerly satisfy every detail. If you know your motivational pattern, you can perceive if your viewpoint is based on motivated inclinations rather than objective principles. Understand how you are inclined to react and then do what you ought to do.

# CHAPTER SEVENTEEN
# Playing to Your Strengths

W E KNOW that each reader has approached this book according to his or her motivational pattern. We realize that each chapter and every exercise is not equally important to all readers. But you may have missed or given inadequate attention to critical information that you'll need to derive the full benefits from your unique design. Because of the fundamental concepts presented in this book, we suggest that you flip through its pages at this time and critique your reading, reviewing material as needed.

We are eager that you leave our company equipped with the self-knowledge necessary to readdress your career, fully realizing its potential to contribute to life's fulfillment. Again, we stress the importance of knowing what you bring to your work and to your many roles in life. Remember the need for discipline in discovering and developing your motivational gifts.

In the end, it makes no difference what color collar you wear as long as your work fits you. If you produce with pleasure and are useful to others, it makes little difference what kinds of tools are required. Whether you work in an office, studio, classroom, factory, laboratory, or in the wilderness is relevant only to the extent that the setting provides the circumstances in which you can apply your motivational abilities.

Finally, you must examine the issue of success and create a personal definition. Your concept may be different than that promoted by society, but when you exercise gifts that have been disciplined and contribute to your full potential, you can be successful whether or not you are famous or rich. This is good simultaneously for you, the organization for which you work, and all others who benefit from the results of your efforts. Such a triple blessing is worth investing our lives.

# Afterword

BEFORE putting our book on the shelf, we would like you to consider some of the fascinating implications of the fact that each person is designed with a unique, complex, irrepressible pattern of giftedness and motivation. Reflect on the fact that your motivational pattern, by its nature, includes both a purpose to fulfill as well as the competencies and drive necessary to achieve that purpose. You have a destiny, a calling, a charge to keep! Meaning is built into your life!

Have you ever thought about the fact that those who pursued their calling have built civilizations? Only the exercise of giftedness and the passion of men and women in past generations seeking to realize their dreams, satisfy their curiosity, and solve the problems of their age has made it all possible. There is no other power accessible to us through which we can compose and paint, invent and discover, design and build, strategize and theorize, sell and entertain. We can't make or develop new giftedness and motivation! Every product, process, system, or recipe that works well; every expression of the human spirit and creativity worthy of praise; every word of healing counsel and act of unfeigned concern; owe the fact of those achievements to unique endowments of those involved.

Through the ages, many respected observers of the human condition noted this presence of a driving excellence. From Plato and Socrates to Swedenborg, Kierkegaard, Jung, and Whitehead, the belief in personal destiny and individual giftedness and motivation has been the subject of much speculation. Shakespeare contributed this inspired poetic insight:

> *There is a history in all men's lives,*
> *Figuring the nature of the times deceased:*
> *The which observed, a man may prophesy,*
> *With a near aim, of the main chance of things*
> *As yet not come to life; which in their seeds,*
> *And weak beginnings, lie intreasured.*

Henry IV

Increasing numbers of contemporary researchers and philosophers have noted a dynamic patterned uniqueness reflected in the behavior of individuals. Many attribute the phenomenon to a slow, lengthy developmental process caused by interaction between unique genetic endowment and environment. Others reason it to be the result, over a period of years, of a person striving to be consistent in behavior. Neither of these mechanisms squares well with facts we have observed and described in these pages (see Chapter 9). In recent years, a few pioneers in relevant fields of inquiry—Allport, Horney, Koestler, Maslow, May, Norton, Polanyi, and Rappaport—have observed or reasoned that there exists within persons a developed and dynamic excellence which seeks expression: a conclusion we would affirm, although we would insert a compelling rationale and force as the source of that excellence.

Because each person's motivated behavior emerges in early childhood in the form of a reasonably well fleshed-out, distinct pattern, it is clearly not the result of a developmental process. Because that motivational pattern appears unique to each person when precisely described, is systemic and cohesive, is essentially fixed and enduring, expresses the irrepressible essence of how the person thinks, speaks, and acts, and because of the pattern's explicit, idiosyncratic purposiveness, we are drawn irresistibly to the notion of detailed design. Detailed design admits, or in our view requires, intentionality. It seems blindly irrational to exclude a numinous cause for the patterned uniqueness of persons. To consider God as designer, actively involved in the unfolding drama of His children, is to us the most reasonable and satisfying explanation for the phenomenon of motivated patterns.

The nature of our relationship with God is a facet of theology affirmed throughout the centuries by theologians who have sought to fathom the unfathomable. Hans Kung, to take one contemporary source for example, observes that

> . . . there is someone who faces us as benevolent and absolutely reliable; not an object, not an empty, unechoing universe, not a merely silent infinite, not an undefinable, nameless Gnostic chasm, not an indeterminate, dark abyss that might be confused with nothingness, still less an anonymous interpersonal something that could be mistaken for man and his very fragile love. God is one who faces me, whom I can address." (Hans Küng, *Does God Exist?* New York: Vantage Press, 1981)

If we allow God to draw us into His embrace, the requirements placed on our part of this deeply personal relationship center in love, we act to serve others using gifts given for that service. Unlike new age mysticism and its antecedent religions, achievement and results are stressed, along with a need to see justice served and to produce fruits from the talents endowed. Craftsmanship, creativity, humbleness, realism, and a belief in the assessment of giftedness are part and parcel of God's requirements. Corrective repentance and sorrow are accessible when error in thought or deed harms others, or thrusts us into pretension, selfishness, cowardice, or self-doubt. Yet, as C.S. Lewis reminded us, joy is the business of heaven. God calls us to build a kingdom on earth as it is in heaven, where we can continue to enjoy using our gifts and their fruit, but sweat and toil.

Holy Scripture abounds in its references to God's involvement in the nature and use of our giftedness. Among our favorites are:

Thou hast ascended on high, thou hast led captivity captive: thou hast received gifts for men: yea, for the rebellious also, that the Lord God might dwell among them. (Psalms 68:18)

We are God's handiwork, created in Christ Jesus, that we should perform the good works for which we were designed. (Ephesians 2:10)

He has filled them with skill to carry out all the crafts of an engraver, damask weaver, embroiderer in purple stuffs, of violet shade and red, in crimson stuffs and fine linen, or of the common weaver; they are able to do work of all kinds and to do it with originality. (Exodus 35:35)

Many years ago, an article in the *Atlantic Monthly* captured this mysterious blending of divine intention and human striving for suitable achievement.

The more normal, expansive mystical experiences come apparently when the personal self is at its best. Its powers and capacities are raised to an unusual unity and fused together. The whole being, with its accumulated submerged life, finds itself. The process of preparing for any high achievement is a severe and laborious one; but nothing seems easier in the moment of success than is the accomplishment for which the life has been prepared. There comes to be formed within the person what Aristotle called "a dexterity of soul," so that the person does with ease what he has become skilled to do. Brother Lawrence finely says: "The most excellent method which I found of going to God was that of doing my common business purely for the love of God." (Rufus Jones, "The Mystics' Experience of God," *Atlantic Monthly*, 1921)

God has given His prized creation the means for personal significance, joy, fulfillment, honor, respect, and beauty, the capacity to love with the whole heart, the whole mind, the whole strength, as gifts are poured out in service to others; and an eternity of delight in the work of our hands.

However, we believe these unsearchable riches contain a "but." The qualifier is that we must live our lives in relationship with God, always remembering we are created and defined by God; that He is God and we are precious but only specks of His expression. It is here that many lose their way.

We have seen, in our 30 years of experience in helping people identify their motivational patterns, how men and women are lured into a false view of themselves. Use of their giftedness gives some people the feeling of a God-like quality or entitlement; e.g., being adored, being exalted, being envied, being seen as special, having others submit to their will, doing things difficult for others to achieve, seeing and experiencing things no one else has discovered, being unique, building monuments to themselves, and so on.

These experiences are heady ones and may lead people to compulsively seek repeat performances. They fail to realize that they can only do what they do because they have been given the means to do so. The power to achieve seduces them into self-deception. As hideous as it is, some prefer power over others to loving others or even being loved by them. But they cannot have both except in the context of an empowering and constraining relationship with God.

Striving to be independent from God, so endemic to the human race, is what the Bible calls sin. Seeking and experiencing achievement is not sin. We were designed for achievement. Sin is denying God as Lord of our lives and refusing to submit to His provisions for and government of our lives. God cannot abide this—He does not intend to run a foot race with anybody.

When we attempt to live without God, the results are disastrous. The dynamics of our giftedness, our fears and insecurities, and the terrible lust for self-determination ultimately seem to lead to self-destruction. Play out the scenario of people who are successful in this life. They become filled with themselves and suffer the psychological torment of protecting and maintaining their treasures of status, track record, and material gains. Some become stressed, leading to an early death or crippling disability. Others who succeed for awhile lose their nerve, falter in their lives, and become less than they might because their confidence in themselves has failed. Still others just bump along in life, never fully aware of their potential, playing it safe, clutching some false security, trying to play it smart, unwilling to trust God and invest their lives in their gifts.

Without God, we are left with our drive to be God. Regardless of how we try to appear, regardless of how well we do, we are left with greed, jealousy, suspicion, unrequitable desire, anxiety, dread, depression, and ugliness.

Breaking into this human dilemma is the person of Jesus Christ, lover of our souls, who empowered men and women by giving them gifts through which they could love a civilization into existence. Tragically, the gifts bestowed on people became the means for them to challenge God, set up their own kingdoms, and inherit the horror of eternity without God.

However, God so loved the world that when confronted by a creation refusing to follow His ground rules, he asked Jesus Christ to atone for the sins of His creation and to free people from the law that said if you sin, you die. Jesus Christ, the Lord of Life, became Saviour of the world. He defeated the law of sin and death . . . weeping . . . bloodied . . . victorious.

At this point, God entered into the affairs of mankind through His Holy Spirit to bring about a redemption of the world built on the person and character of Jesus Christ. To those who invite God into their hearts, His Holy Spirit is literally resident within them to work out God's intention to redeem that part of the world in which they labor.

Nothing is left out. All can be redeemed. Every detail of life can be brought into the light of worked-out faith, regardless of whether it is a scientist trying to make sense of contradiction in observed data, a marketeer prophetically planning next decade's products, a poet struggling to tease out an illusive image, or a third baseman recovering confidence after an error.

Faith in God can always lead to a personal working relationship where we can rely on Him to enter into the details of our lives; where He will instruct us when we need help, admonish us when we get out of line, encourage us when we are fearful, and delight us with personal expressions of His love. There may be problems, sacrifice, pain, and sorrow, but there is always joy at the end of the trial. Through these transactions, God helps us mature, leading us to the particular fullness of expression and fruit bearing He had in mind when He designed us.

For sheer pleasure, a powerful sense of meaning, direction and yet profound freedom, nothing can compare to a life worshipping God by doing what you were designed to do, knowing that God is in charge and responsible for the results.

So why all this God stuff?

We want you to look hard at the apparent fact you literally are designed with a destiny to find and fulfill.

We want you to consider seriously the possibility that God is your author and wants to be involved in how you work out the details of your life.

We want you to seek to know God in the same way you seek to know any person or subject important to you, reading, discussing, listening, doing, trying. Confront God with your curiosity or your hurt or your sin. You may find helpful a book about a theology of work we wrote called *Finding A Job You Can Love* (Thomas Nelson, 1982). It may help provide a base for understanding applied faith in real-life terms.

Don't worry about whether God will do His part. You are His idea and He knows how to make connection with you.

And finally, when you do connect, do three things: Spend time with God in a way natural to you, soak up lots of Scripture, and get close to other seeking Christians.

Arthur F. Miller
Ralph T. Mattson

# APPENDIX

## SIMA# - BIOGRAPHICAL INFORMATION FORM

This following form is provided to help you discover your motivated abilities. It is illegal to reproduce the form without written permission. Professionals interested in incorporating the SIMA#process into their work or into corporate human resource functions can write People Management, Inc., 10 Station Street, Simsbury, CT 06070 for information or the address of our nearest office or affiliate currently in St. Paul, MN, Atlanta, GA, Pittsburgh, PA, Oxford, England, or Wellington, New Zealand.

Name _____

Address _____

_____
City                State              Zip
Phone _____

Date _____

# SIMA®
# BIOGRAPHICAL FORM

# PEOPLE MANAGEMENT

INCORPORATED

10 STATION STREET SIMSBURY, CONN. 06070 203 651-3581

# System for Identifying Motivated Abilities
## before you start

If you are like most people, you have never taken time to sort out the things you are good at and motivated to accomplish. As a result, it is unlikely that you use these talents as completely or effectively as you could.

Identification of your strengths and vocationally significant motivations is the purpose of SIMA.®

To complete this form, you are asked to list and describe things you have done that you:
                    1) enjoyed doing      and .· 2) believed you did well.
Such achievement activities may have occurred in your work or your home life or your leisure time.

It is imperative that you put down what was important to you. Do not include an item only because others felt it was important. The activities you list may be quite simple and not impressive to others. They may have nothing to do with success, great accomplishments, fame or fortune. Concentrate on activities that gave YOU a sense of satisfaction. They may have made you feel proud. They may have been just plain fun ·ᴏ do. They may have been a combination of pleasure and pain, but they left you feeling fulfilled, a ᴀomplished, proud or otherwise satisfied.

Also, it is esential that you relate specific achievement activities and not general ones. To help you understand the type of achievement activities we are after, you will find below examples of things other people have listed as personally significant.

You will have the opportunity to develop a similar list on pages 5, 6, and 7.

## summary examples

"Putting on plays for neighborhood children with costumes, props, etc. The most successful project was transforming a shed in back of our house into a fairyland with lighting effects, decorations, princesses."

"I built and mastered the tallest pair of stilts in my neighborhood. I started a stilt craze among my friends."

"I had a job as a printer's devil. I developed a method of cutting stereotypes which was faster and more accurate than that previously used."

"I established an evening routine of a quiet time of sharing and reading with our children which made bedtime an enjoyable end to the day.

"Was a prime mover in starting company. Saw utility of product concept. Had much to do with early market development. Helped conceive basic manufacturing concepts."

"Organized and ran a company-sponsored national conference with about 100 participants. Conference was a resounding success."

"Won the support of my subordinates over a period of years by building strong relationships. Took an interest in developing careers, always sent cards on birthdays, Christmas and special events."

It is easy to misunderstand these examples. If you review them again, you will discover that they are:

- Achievement Activities, Not Experiences
- Specific Activities, Not Milestone Achievements
- Activities You Can Support with Examples

By way of explanation, we will contrast good examples with poor ones.

### Achievement Activities, Not Experiences

Not: "I toured Europe with my wife and the Alps were beautiful."
But: "I fixed a grandfather's clock when I was 12 years old that hadn't worked for 2 years."

### Specific Activities, Not Milestone Achievements

Not: "Got my Ph.D." or "Had a baby" or "Became Operations Manager."
But: "Made original discoveries in science labs" or "Coached my wife during childbirth" or "Worked with subordinates to improve their skills; improved output by 25%."

### Activities You Can Support with Examples

Not: "I'm good at troubleshooting."
But: "Caught a design problem during prototype testing and saved the company over $10,000.'

Before you begin to write, read the following principles and tips carefully.

# TIPS FOR COMPLETING THIS FORM

- Take enough time to complete the form. On the average, it takes between 2 and 6 hours

- Don't worry about whether or not you can recall impressive childhood achievements. Select any activity you can remember enjoying and doing well. Don't reject it because it seems silly, trivial or unimportant.

- Write what was important to you, not what was important to your family or to your friends. If some honor or recognition left you cold, leave it out.

- Don't be limited to narrow time frames. If you have enjoyed achievement activities that have occurred over a stretch of years, list them in the long term (LT) section. If you're proud of them and enjoyed the activity, it's worth documenting.

- If you want more space, take it. Add pages if necessary.

- If your activities occurred in a group setting, and you did nothing different from the others, describe what all of you did.

- When you recall something you did and believe you did well, write it down. Don't try to analyze or evaluate it. We're looking for your history, not your evaluation. The analysis is our job.

- Don't be modest. You are the key actor in every event. These are *your* achievements.

# THE THREE STEPS

There are three steps in completing this form. The better you complete each one, the more you will enhance our ability to provide you with an accurate description of your Motivated Abilities:

<u>Step 1</u>  Write a summary of your achievement activities. In other words, a list of brief descriptions.

<u>Step 2</u>  Select eight of the most important activities from the summary list.

<u>Step 3</u>  Write one-page expansions on each of the selected eight.

Remember, there is no time limit to complete the form. IT IS NOT A TEST, so enjoy yourself. There are no right or wrong answers.

## STEP 1

# SUMMARY OF ACHIEVEMENT ACTIVITIES

For each period, briefly describe two or more specific things you accomplished that you enjoyed doing and believed you did well. If it would be helpful, put the calendar years covered under the age period: i.e., "'49-'53" — create additional categories for more achievements if you wish to add (a-3, b-3, etc.). If you wish to note long-term achievements, place them under the LT designation at the end of this section.

Childhood
(a-1)

(a-2)

Teen Years *(If you are in this age group, continue listing examples, ignoring the age categories.)*
(b-1)

(b-2)

Age _____
(c-1)

(c-2)

Age _____
(d-1)


(d-2)


Age _____
(e-1)


(e-2)


Age _____
(f-1)


( f-2)

Age _____
(g-1)


(g-2)


Age _____
(h-1)


(h-2)


<u>Long-Term Achievement Activities</u>

(LT-1)


(LT-2)


(LT-3)

STEP 2

## SELECTING

Of the things you have described, note in the boxes below the eight that are particularly important to you (e.g., b-2, f-1), not necessarily in order of importance. Please place an asterisk* next to the summary achievement activities (in step 1) you have chosen. If possible, try to pick examples from your whole life, not just recent activities.

□    □    □    □    □    □    □    □

## STEP 3

# EXPANDING ON THE MOST IMPORTANT ACHIEVEMENT ACTIVITIES

Taking the eight most important activities in the order given in the preceding boxes, describe:

1. How you got involved in it;
2. The details of what you actually did (elaborate and expand); and,
3. What was particularly enjoyable or satisfying to you.

Some individuals like to write, so they will thoroughly enjoy this exercise. Others are reluctant to do this much writing. If you are in the latter category, you might dictate your expansion into a tape recorder and have someone transcribe your words onto the following pages.

Try to fill each page, focusing on the details of what you actually did.

Start each page by repeating the summary statement about the achievement.

# SAMPLE EXPANSION

---

<u>achievement activity</u> ( E~1  )  **3**

One line summary statement: *Purchased And Renovated A rundown 2 family house; doubled its value; Made it a nice place to Live.*

How you got involved: *Read a book that said the best way to buy property, was to selectively buy rundown multi-family housing And renovate*

Details of what you did (how you actually went about doing it):
*Read the book mentioned Above; set out to find A house that met the requirements. Found it and negotiated a good purchase price. I then gave the upstairs tenants notice to leave and started to rebuild the porches, paint the house and clean up the yard. Meanwhile, I reassured the downstairs tenants that they would not have to move.*

*When the upstairs tenants were gone I proceeded to renovate the upstairs apt. Partly with my own labor — partly with contractors*

*The goal was to create a pleasant place for me and my family to live with rental income to offset some of the cost. In Addition, I wanted to get personal experience doing this kind of work both by myself and thru contractors and, to end up with a property that had increased equity to fund future investments*

What was particularly satisfying to you:
*I accomplished this goal as planned*

## <u>achievement activity</u> ( ) 1

One line summary statement:

How you got involved:

Details of what you did (how you actually went about doing it):

What was particularlv satisfying to you:

## <u>achievement activity</u> (      ) 2

One line summary statement:

How you got involved:

Details of what you did (how you actually went about doing it):

What was particularly satisfying to you:

## <u>achievement activity</u> (      ) 3

One line summary statement:

How you got involved:

Details of what you did (how you actually went about doing it):

What was particularly satisfying to you:

## achievement activity (          )  **4**

One line summary statement:

How you got involved:

Details of what you did (how you actually went about doing it)

What was particularly satisfying to you:

## <u>achievement activity</u> (          )  5

One line summary statement:

How you got involved:

Details of what you did (how you actually went about doing it):

What was particularly satisfying to you:

## <u>achievement activity</u> ( ) 6

One line summary statement:

How you got involved:

Details of what you did (how you actually went about doing it):

What was particularly satisfying to you:

## <u>achievement activity</u> (        ) 7

One line summary statement:

How you got involved:

Details of what you did (how you actually went about doing it):

What was particularly satisfying to you:

## <u>achievement activity</u> (      ) 8

One line summary statement:

How you got involved:

Details of what you did (how you actually went about doing it):

What was particularly satisfying to you:

## work chronology

| dates | organization | title-function |
|-------|-------------|----------------|
|       |             |                |
|       |             |                |
|       |             |                |
|       |             |                |
|       |             |                |
|       |             |                |
|       |             |                |

**EDUCATION SUMMARY**

College - Year - Degree - Major

Graduate Work

Activities

Favorite Subjects - College                    H.S.

**SPARE TIME INFORMATION**

What activities give you most pleasure outside of work?


When you were a child?

"... the gift of administration (should be used) in administration. A teacher should employ his gift in teaching, and one who has the gift of stirring speech should use it to stir his hearers. If you give to charity, give with all your heart; if you are a leader, exert yourself to lead..."

Romans 12: 7-9 NEB